Tales from W

Tales from West Yorkshire

~

Leonard Markham

With illustrations by Don Osmond

COUNTRYSIDE BOOKS
NEWBURY, BERKSHIRE

First published in 1992
© Leonard Markham 1992

COUNTRYSIDE BOOKS
3 CATHERINE ROAD
NEWBURY, BERKSHIRE

ISBN 1 85306 190 5

Produced through MRM Associates Ltd., Reading
Typeset by Wessex Press Design & Print Ltd., Warminster
Printed by J. W. Arrowsmith Ltd., Bristol

For Douglas and Shirley

Shake a bridle over a Yorkshireman's grave and he will arise and steal a horse.

Old proverb

Contents

YORKSHIRE — The map overleaf is by John Speede and shows the area as it was in the early seventeenth century

DIEU ET MON DROIT

THE GER
MAIN
OCEAN

EAST

NORTH RIDING
LANGBARGH WAPONTAK
RYDALE WAPENTAKE
PICKERING WAPENT
Blakey More
Cleve Lande

Guiburgh
Whitby
Scarbrough

PICKERING FOREST
Pickering Lithe
DICKERING

New Malton
BUCCROSSE WAPON
YORKE WOULD
EAST
Bridlington
Kilham
THE WAPO

YORKE
OUSE
LAND
DARWET
WAP
RIDING
DIGHTON

Wighton
HART
Beverley

HOWDEN
WAPON
HOLDERNESSE
WAP

Marshe Lande
Diche Marche
Hull
Humber Flu
WAPON
Burton

PART OF
Æxholme
Iland
STRASFORTH
AND
Doncaster
LINCOLNE

WAPON

PART OF NOT
TINGAM
SHIRE
Blythe
SHIRE

PRIVSEGO.

THE SCALE OF MILES
1 2 3 4 5 6 7 8 9 10 11 12 13 14 15 16

The Jolly Post-Boy

The old coaching days in Yorkshire are a fount of wonderful tales, the romantically dubbed 'flyers' — the Comet, Peveril of the Peak and Tally Ho! — conjuring Pickwickian images of stove-pipe hats and hot nags. The exploits of the coach drivers and highwaymen like Dick Turpin are well known, but what of the antics of the post-boys with their 'white chokers, gorgeous waistcoats and wondrous pearl buttons'? Theirs is a no less rumbustious story.

Post-boys (even old timers were so called) were almost as indispensable as the horse in England's transport system before the arrival of the railways. Gaudily dressed, shod with yellow topped boots and accoutred with a false leg made of leather and iron which was worn on the off-side leg as a protection against the chafing of the carriage pole, Yorkshire post-boys plied their trade day and night between great staging posts such as Ferrybridge, Wetherby, Bradford and Leeds, sometimes travelling hundreds of miles at a stretch. Principally responsible for riding postillion, for assisting passengers, paying toll fees and returning horses to their home stables, post-boys had to provide their own clothing, and although they received board and lodging from their masters, they were paid no wages, relying solely for their living on tips.

11

Characterful rogues, 'many of them being of very diminutive stature, with shrivelled-up figures, quaint, wrinkled faces, and a quiet, knowing eye, the body stooping forward, and a constant drooping at the knee, as though they were continuously in the saddle', these Tykes were distinguished by fellows like George Barker and Tom Groom of the Angel in Ferrybridge. Theirs was an arduous and often dangerous job — cantankerous horses, appalling road conditions, the scourge of the highwaymen, the violent nature of some of their passengers and the obvious temptations of the wayside inn, making for an exciting life.

The fortitude and good nature of the post-boys, who were 'as fond of their joke and as full of rollicking fun as the roads were full of ruts', is well illustrated by an incident which took place at the famous Angel.

One black night, a gentleman's carriage arrived outside the inn. Fresh horses were harnessed and the post-boy, George Barker, prepared for departure.

'I say, George!' shouted the lad who had escorted the sole passenger along the preceding stage. 'You've got a rum customer inside. He won't settle up for the journey; he'll neither pay me nor the bars, nor yet for the horses; he's had his pistols out all along the road swearing he'd shoot me. He's a rum 'un he is. He'll blow a hole through you before you get to Doncaster!'

Scoffing, smiling, dismissing the warning as a joke, our post-boy set out in high spirits, but before he left the town he had a shock.

'Damn you, drive faster, or I'll put a bullet through you!' shrieked a voice.

The imperturbable George responded with coolness. 'All right sir, fast enough after a bit, sir.' But the passenger, irritable and impatient, unleashed a stream of profanities all the way up Darrington Hill, threatening the post-boy and vowing that he would not have a farthing for him or his steeds.

The pistols were cocked and George feared for his life, deciding that his tormentor was either mad or drunk. Pulling off the road into a deep valley below Wentbridge Hill, he decided to confront his man. (Men of this county will spit in the eye of the Devil if brass is at stake.)

'Well, if I'm not to be paid, I don't go any further,' insisted George.

'Drive on at once, you ---- rascal or I'll shoot you instantly.'

'Shoot away, but I'm not going back wi' my horses.'

The resolution of George and the prospect of spending a cold night in the ravine eased the traveller's temper. He calmed down, put his weapons to one side and parleyed, promising to pay his dues at the next staging post in Doncaster. The journey continued with mild complaints and growls.

Eventually, the carriage reached its destination and drew up at the New Angel inn.

'Why the devil have you stopped here?' asked the traveller. 'Go across the road to the other house.'

'But this is my usual house.'

'Don't talk to me, you villain; go to the Old Angel at once.' George complied with the instructions, much to the annoyance of the innkeeper.

Having attended to the horses, ever determined, George then marched to the traveller's room, the verbal battle resuming in a blaze of anger and swearing. Consuming liquor at gunpoint, George persevered. The traveller finally relented and paid for the horses, but adamantly refused to offer anything for George himself. 'You scoundrel, I'll give you nothing for yourself. Have another glass.'

'No, thank you sir.'

'Have another glass, you ----- villain, or I'll shoot you.'

Between gulps, George kept repeating his demands to be paid . . . and persistence triumphed in the end. George later recounted his adventure to astonished friends.

'I hed all sorts o' glasses. He gev me alf-a soverayn at the finish. I nivver wor so filled up i' all my life afore. I fell off seven times between Doncaster an' York Bar, an' then I fell asleep in t'hedge bottom, an lost one o' t'horses.'

'Eh! he wor a terrible customer wor that thear, bud I stuck to him an' got my brass after all.'

> ' Three jolly postboys drinking at the Dragon,
> And they determined to finish out the flagon.
>
> Punch cures gout, the colic and the phithisic,
> And it is allowed to be the very best of physic.
>
> Landlord fill the bowl till it does flow over,
> For there's not a jolly soul that goes to bed sober.
>
> He that drinks and goes to bed sober,
> Falls as the leaves and dies in October.
>
> He that drinks and goes to bed mellow,
> Lives as he ought to live, and dies a jolly fellow.'

Mister Chips

Hot, golden, and scrumptious, fish and chips vie with Yorkshire pudding for our county's culinary crown. Despite the advent of fast food, the corner chippy prospers, offering an unassailably nutritious and delicious meal at the keenest of prices. Part of the fabric of West Yorkshire life, these inspirations for all take-away food shops have had millions of devotees over the years. Perhaps the most inspirational was Henry Ramsden's famous emporium at Guiseley near Leeds.

All West Yorkshire folk will be familiar with the Harry Ramsden's restaurant. Dubbed 'the biggest fish and chip shop in the world' this establishment, complete with modern ranges, furnishings, and crystal chandeliers, continues its proud traditions, honouring its pioneering founder.

The story of Harry Ramsden rightly begins with his father, who from modest beginnings created the fish and chip empire at the turn of the century in Bradford. Young Harry was one of several chips off the old block who were destined for stardom, nephew Harry Corbett and the glove puppet Sooty also becoming household names.

Employing a coal fired range in one of Bradford's poorer districts, Harry senior was a hard working disciplinarian who expected his offspring to help with the chores. Harry junior, however, had different ideas. A rebellious and determined individual, he set his own erratic course, becoming in turn, a lather-boy in a barber's shop, a telegram delivery boy and a taxi proprietor, using a private loan to fund the business. During these impressionable years he accepted an important maxim which was to stand him in good stead for all his subsequent ventures: 'always pay your debts when they are due'.

In 1911, at the tender age of 21, Harry decided to become the landlord of the Craven Heifer in Bradford, and he approached his father for a loan. Rejected with the remark 'I'll lend thee enough to see a doctor to 'ave thi' 'ead examined . . . thinkin' of takin' a pub at 21!' but undeterred, Harry secured a bank loan, and went on to convert the fortunes of the previously mediocre pub by demonstrating his flair for hospitality and by providing the novel attraction of a piano.

The First World War interrupted a promising career. After his national service, Harry shunned the licensed trade and took up the filleting knife, opening his first fish and chip shop at the Wibsey Fair, and then moving on to other successful premises at the corner of Manchester Road and Bower Street. What customer service! This shop was open every lunchtime, every tea-time, and every night for 365 days a year, including Christmas Day!

A second shop was acquired in Westgate and the business burgeoned with expansion into the next door property. Decorated with trade-mark hunting prints and chequered tiles, the converted Cosy Cafe attracted a wide clientele, including members of the theatrical profession. Harry's wife Beatrice ran a boarding house for actors and comedians and the latter helped promote the Cosy Cafe by referring to it on stage. Although the next five years were financially successful, they were marred by the declining health of Beatrice. After the birth of a son in 1924, Beatrice contracted tuberculosis. Harry moved the family to more salubrious surroundings in White Cross, buying a wooden lock-up shop to continue his business. Unfortunately, Beatrice died in 1929 and never saw the 200 seater restaurant that Harry built near their cottage.

Opened in 1931, at a time of chronic unemployment, the new venture initially relied on bulk outsales to working class customers, but was soon expanded to cater for more affluent diners. Ever a perfectionist, Harry pursued the goal of quality at every turn, insisting that the weight of ingredients for the closely guarded batter recipe should be accurate to within one grain, and that battered fish should be fried for exactly two and a half minutes each side. Ranges and chip buckets were built to his exact specifications, a metal base on castors was specially designed to aid the movement of the cumbersome chip tubs, and innovative use was made of stainless steel to ensure hygienic working conditions. A stickler for cleanliness, Harry searched diligently for a char lady who could match his own exacting standards. A Mrs Ineson was put to the test. 'Watch this,' insisted an unseen Harry dropping a match onto the floor. 'She won't miss it.' The match was duly whisked into the dustpan and Harry beamed.

Lavishing the same attention to detail on the restaurant, Harry replaced the original rubberoid floor with wall to wall carpet, installed elegant chandeliers, provided music and facilities for snooker, and even consulted a team of experts to solve the age old conundrum of the dripping teapot. He had less success with his name-stamped cutlery, eager visitors purloining the knives and forks as souvenirs. The wide-eyed reaction of customers can be appreciated by the comments of a small boy who asked his father '. . . is this where God comes for his fish and chips?'

A complex, self effacing character with many friends in the world of entertainment, Harry was renowned for being the archetypal Yorkshireman. He had slot machines fitted to the restaurant walls and delighted at the loss of each penny. The annoying habit of visitors to his coin operated toilets (some left the doors ajar and allowed the next person a free turn!) had a corresponding opposite effect. And Harry was constantly alive to the minor pilfering of staff. On one occasion, he spied the tail of a plaice protruding from an employee's jacket which had been left in the cloakroom. Surreptitiously, he removed the fish and replaced it with the contents of the filleting bucket, filling all the pockets for good measure. The thefts stopped without a word.

A born entrepreneur and showman, Harry devised many methods of boosting sales. He provided a variety of live entertainment for restaurant customers and behind his premises he regularly organised fairs in the summer months, particularly to attract families. He arranged brass band concerts for older customers and offered a fish and chip delivery service targeted on

18

mill workers. Business boomed and although Harry lost money on other speculative investments, particularly in trying to develop local dance halls, he became rich and was recognised as one of the most generous and best loved characters in West Yorkshire.

On 7th July 1952, despite continuing post-war rationing, the White Cross restaurant celebrated its 21st birthday in grand style, tantalising customers with fish and chips at 1912 prices, as an acknowledgement to Ramsden's modest beginnings. Thousands of people queued to buy fish and chips for a penny ha'-penny and a magnificent day was crowned with entertainment by Harry Corbett and a firework display. This was to be Harry Ramsden's last extravaganza.

In 1954, feeling the strain of running such a demanding business, Harry opted for semi-retirement, leaving the operation of the White Cross restaurant to colleagues. Typically, he immediately opened a new fish and chip shop in Shipley. This was shortly followed by the acquisition of a second shop in Wetherby. But illness had taken its toll. Cancer was diagnosed. Refusing a life-saving operation, Harry Ramsden spent months fighting the disease, finally succumbing on 7th January 1963. The perfect epitaph to a remarkable Yorkshireman was provided by the *Telegraph and Argus*:

Goodbye Mr Chips

Harry stood at the Pearly Gate,
His face was worn and old,
He meekly asked the man of fate,

19

Admission to the fold.
'What have you done' old Peter asked,
'to seek admittance here?'
'I owned a Guiseley Fish Shop
For many and many a year.'
The gate flew open sharply, as
Peter touched the bell,
'Come in old man, and take a harp,
You've had enough of Hell. . .'

The Murder
of
Robin Hood

R obin Hood was indubitably a Yorkshireman.
Suggest that England's favourite outlaw hailed
from Nottingham and receive a shaft between the
eyes!

Ancient tales suggest that Robin was born of yeoman
stock in the town of Wakefield, and that he spent some
of his time in the Barnsdale and Wentbridge areas,
waylaying travellers near the valley of the river Went.
Of his adventures much has been written, his crusades
against oppression and his rollicking life in the
greenwood enriching the folklore of England more
than any other exploits in history. His 'life' is well
chronicled in myriad pamphlets and books, but what
of his death?

In 1247, to Kirklees Priory, a Cistercian nunnery
near Mirfield, came an indisposed Robin Hood,
escorted by his faithful companion Little John.
Repairing to the gatehouse, Robin was treated by the
sisters of mercy, with dire results. The malevolent
prioress, Elizabeth de Stainton, prescribed

venesection — the panacea for all ills. An artery was deliberately severed, and Robin began to bleed to death. Realising that the end was near, Robin took his bugle horn and trumpeted 'weak blasts three'. Little John answered the call and rushed to the sound.

'Bring me my bow and let me shoot once more!' implored Robin.

'At what would you shoot?' asked Little John.

'My grave dear friend! Bury me wherever this arrow falls.' With failing strength the shaft was loosed, and some hours later, Robin's life ebbed away.

> 'And where this arrow is taken up,
> There shall my grave digged be,
> Lay me a green sod under my head,
> And another at my feet.
>
> 'And lay my bent bow by my side
> Which was my music sweet,
> And make my grave of gravel and green,
> Which is most right and meet.
>
> 'Let me have length and breadth enough
> With a green sod under my head;
> That they may say, when I am dead,
> Here lies bold Robin Hood.'

What motivated the murder of Robin Hood? The murderess, we are told, was a kinswoman, Robin's evil aunt who was inflamed by suggestions of her nephew's opposition to the religious orders. Acting with her lover accomplice, the priest, Sir Roger of Doncaster, the lady carried out her evil act and quickly fled the wrath of Little John, who in a fit of anger cursed the priory for ever.

In later years, the accursed priory became an even viler den of iniquity, reports circulating of orgies, 'allurements of the flesh', and of clergy and laymen being welcomed into 'secret places'. In 1539, the infamous house was dissolved by Henry VIII, and its stones were dismantled and plundered for the building of the nearby Kirklees Hall. The rebuilt gatehouse where the hero was treacherously slain, and his rude grave on the hillside overlooking the river Calder, remain as the most tantalising evidence of the legend of Robin Hood.

Mouldering in a private estate, having lain for centuries beneath a shroud of intertwining ivy and weeds, Robin's exact place of interment remains conjecture. In the 18th century, estate owner Sir Samuel Armytage attempted an exhumation of the marked grave, but he found nothing, and more modern researchers have been denied entry. Radiating a mystical aura, the grave has long attracted the attention of spiritualists and those with an interest in the occult. Continually venerated as a shrine, the simple gravestone was desecrated in the early 19th century during the construction of the Lancashire and Yorkshire Railway. Navvies invested the slab with curative properties, chipping off pieces to place under their pillows to alleviate toothache! Other visitations have had more macabre aims. The site is reputed to have been the venue for black rituals and devil worship, and there are stories of vampires and hauntings. And there have been a series of unexplained murders and tragic accidents in the vicinity, prompting the explanation that Little John's curse is active still.

The Yorkshire Robin Hood Society are, meanwhile, pressing for public access to what should be a nationally important site, and for a proper Christian burial for the prince amongst thieves . . . a proper Yorkshireman . . . the hero of England's most stirring ballad. . . .

> 'No archer like him was so good,
> His wildness called him Robin Hood.
> For thirteen years and somewhat more
> These nothern parts he vexed sore;
> Such outlaws as he and his men
> May England never know again.'

The Hermit
of Rombald's Moor

The wild and windswept bogs and crags on
Rombald's Moor between Ilkley and Keighley
present an eerie landscape, pock-marked with
strangely inscribed stones, cairns, hut-circles, field
systems, barrows, entrenchments and enclosures.
Evidence of lost civilisations is etched all around, and
visitors have journeyed here for centuries to commune
with the mystic past. In the early 1800s, however, they
came to consult another oracle, a hermit who lived in a
tumble-down shack in Burley Woodhead and who was
an expert on romance and the weather!

Job Senior was born a bastard around 1780, the son
of a wealthy Ilkley landowner. Job lived in the spa town
with his mother, and although little is known of the
lad's upbringing, he is said to have been a robust youth
with a ready wit.

Job's first paid employment was as an itinerant
labourer, travelling between farmsteads as a dry-stone
waller or a wool-comber, earning meagre wages which
barely covered his needs. But then Fate dealt a
generous hand. The death bed contrition of his father
and the bequeathing of a considerable legacy, enabled
Job to lead a dissolute life and to indulge his passion

for strong ale, and he became a regular bar fly, hovering between taverns in Leeds and Skipton. In Leeds, he pursued aspirations of marrying a local girl. The lady spurned his proposals, he resumed his alcoholic sprees and was soon penniless.

Unable to maintain any regular occupation, the poverty stricken Job, who was by now a down at heel vagrant racked by rheumatics, took to slaking his thirst by singing, using his remarkable talent to entertain playhouse audiences in Leeds and Bradford. Encouraged by his success, he once again contemplated tying the knot, this time to an octogenarian whose ownership of a well furnished cottage guaranteed a comfortable retirement to her widower. Swooning with flattery, convinced that the rose had not yet lost its blush, and persuaded that a husband would be an asset around the house, the old lady offered her hand and the couple were wed.

Alas, married bliss lasted but a short time. The old lady quickly died and Job was heart-broken. He became a colourful topic of conversation, pundits theorising on the demise of his dear departed. Accidental death was the verdict of some. Others suggested that the deceased had been over enthusiastically treated by Job for a throat infection, the prescription of boiling hot fat leading to an agonising end. Yet a third opinion postulated death by scalding. Concerned at the threat of hypothermia, Job was alleged to have dug a fireside pit to accommodate his recumbent spouse. An accidentally overturned cauldron of bubbling stew is said to have ensured a fatal warmth.

Job's sorrow grew worse. Irate relatives of the bride

discovered that Job would be the sole beneficiary of the will, and they descended on the marital home, seized everything of value and smashed the place to pieces.

From the debris, Job built himself a makeshift shelter no bigger than a dog kennel. Creeping about on all fours, he became a spectacle of the degenerate man, and sightseers travelled from far and wide to see the wild creature who hereafter became known as the Hermit of Rombald's Moor.

Job was sustained mainly by an adjacent vegetable plot and by money raised by his itinerant singing. He toured the district, an instantly recognisable character in the attire of the meanest tramp. Sporting a mass of patches, his legs wrapped in straw to keep out the cold, with more straw sprouting from his sockless clogs, he hobbled along with the aid of two sticks, a tobacco pipe hanging ridiculously from a string attached to his hat.

As with every eccentric, Job attracted a good deal of criticism and scorn, particularly from jibing children. He was, however, highly regarded as a soothsayer, especially on affairs of the heart and on meteorological matters.

Love-smitten suitors would ask him for advice, and his standard reply, welling from the vastness of his own experience, was to denigrate marriage, pointing to his own unfortunate state. Is it any wonder that bachelorhood prospered in Burley Woodhead?

Prognostications on the weather were of greater note, consulters ignoring his warnings at their peril. His forecasts of a storm, on one occasion, failed to alert the villagers, and there was much damage to local houses. Job's own stoutly secured hovel withstood the blast!

Approaching his 80th year without any easing of the dourness of his outdoor life, Job succumbed to illness whilst on a walking tour. He returned to Ilkley, calling on the way at a Silsden inn to drink an elixiral pint. Its usual efficacy failed, although there were allegations that Job's enemies, detecting the symptoms of a killer disease, drugged his ale to deter recovery. Eventually diagnosed as suffering from cholera, Job sought refuge in a hay barn, but his condition deteriorated and he was taken to a workhouse where he died.

He was buried in the cemetery in Burley in Wharfedale. Fittingly for a man who from puberty discovered the delights of the bar maid's apron, he is remembered in an inn. Job Senior is regularly toasted in The Hermit in Burley Woodhead.

The Factory King

September 1830. 'Yorkshire Slavery' reads a minor headline in the *Leeds Mercury*. The banner introduces an incendiary letter describing the brutal conditions afflicting child mill workers, igniting a storm of controversy that will rage for 17 years.

The author of the letter was Leeds businessman Richard Oastler, a devout Wesleyan and an admirer of William Wilberforce, with a reputation for honesty and missionary zeal. Aware of the plight of the poor through his wholesale grocery business, during a typhus epidemic, Oastler with two friends 'went into the filthiest and most loathsome hovels of the poor, nursed the sick, soothed the dying and fed the convalescent', developing a passion for alleviating suffering that was all consuming.

Following the post-Napoleonic war depression, Oastler was declared bankrupt, eventually succeeding, after his father's death, to the position of land agent to Thomas Thornhill's Fixby Hall estate near Huddersfield. A successful and tireless landlord, a genial and warmhearted convert to the Tory cause, Oastler became involved in politics, always alert to injustice, and always striving to improve the fortunes of his tenants. Such were the calls on his practical skills, that he opened a part-time land agents office in

Halifax, the enterprise blossoming and signalling a bright commercial future, until a fateful meeting with a friend changed his life.

Bradford mill owner John Wood, a leading industrialist employing over 500 men, women and children in his spinning business, exposed his soul, revealing to Oastler his concerns for the exploited masses. Admitting that seven year old 'pieceners' were employed for up to 17 hours per day, that they were flogged for lateness and idleness, and that they were sometimes plunged into vats of icy water to ward off sleep, Wood inspired his astounded friend, the two men making a vow that was to change the English social scene. 'I have had no sleep tonight', declared Wood. 'I cannot allow you to leave me without a pledge that you will use all your influence in trying to remove the cruelties that are practised in our mills!' With his hand on the Bible, Oastler records that he promised 'that I would do what I could. I felt that we were each of us in the presence of the Highest and that the vow was recorded in Heaven.'

Most mill owners deplored Mr Oastler's 'inflammatory letter' but consciences had been pricked. Some mill owners showed genuine concern and the radical MP John Hobhouse quickly introduced a Parliamentary Bill proposing that the employment in the mills of children under the age of nine should be outlawed, and that the working day of minors between the ages of nine and 18 should be restricted to eleven and a half hours. The Bill polarized attitudes and expectations were high, but before it could be enacted, Parliament was dissolved.

Gingered into action, concerned mill owners

formed 'Short Time Committees' and with Oastler as their leader, Fixby Hall became a centre for a campaign aimed at a shorter working day and an improvement in working conditions. Meetings were held throughout the Ridings. With impassioned eloquence, Oastler gave graphic accounts of the savagery of some mill owners, describing the treatment of little girls who were scourged with the lash. Devoting much of his energy, time and personal income to the crusade, Oastler and his friends succeeded in propelling the so called Ten Hours Bill to a second House of Commons reading in 1832. To galvanise public opinion a pilgrimage was organised, contingents from every Yorkshire town marching to York to declare a solemn oath that 'Our children shall be free!' Twenty-five thousand marchers attended the gathering in appalling weather, cheered on the way by supporting crowds. But again the efforts came to nought. Parliament refused to be influenced by the demonstration and the Bill was shelved, the matter being referred to a special committee which was never convened.

Despite further petitions and attempts at parliamentary reform, little progress was made and Oastler was driven to anger. Denouncing the mill owners and even threatening sabotage if the Ten Hours Bill was not supported, he alienated his former associates. He became ill, lost his position at Fixby Hall and for a time was threatened with outright ruin. A spontaneous display of public admiration by 15,000 supporters restored his faith and gave him new hope. Escorted in grand procession, feted by banner waving, cheering crowds with massed bands in the vanguard playing 'See The Conquering Hero Comes', Oastler was applauded all the way to Huddersfield where a rally of over 50,000 people paid testimony to his work. His former employer was, however, less pleased. In pique he accused Oastler of embezzling estate money. Although the charge was later dropped, a minor misdemeanour involving debt arrears resulted in Oastler being sent to the Debtors Prison. Oastler spent his time publishing a magazine called the *Fleet Papers* as friends agitated on his behalf, launching a liberation fund to ensure his speedy return to the fray. Two years of intercession and fund raising secured his release. In failing health, he returned home to a hero's welcome, *The Times* recording the event in a leader headed 'The Ransomed Patriot'. Supported by *The Times*, the proponents of the Ten Hours Bill fought on, the presence of the white-haired Oastler at rallies giving rise to spontaneous applause. But incredibly, the Bill was spurned again by the House of Commons.

Yet another campaign was organised, Oastler suppressing the anguish of losing his wife to join in the debates. In a whirlwind tour lasting three weeks, he visited Yorkshire, Lancashire and Scotland, using all his powers of persuasion to endorse the Bill. The crucial vote came in May 1847. Hearing the momentous news, MPs knelt in thanksgiving.

Working in London, Oastler maintained his battles against exploitation for the remainder of his life, editing a magazine called *The Home* for five years. Longing to visit his beloved Yorkshire at the age of 72, he headed north, dying as he approached Harrogate from a heart attack.

Battling against greed, intolerance and vile

contempt for the sufferings of the mill workers, Richard Oastler secured a brighter future for his little 'pieceners'. Small wonder that to this day he is known as 'The Factory King'.

Barwick's
Ancient Maypole

The royal capital of the extensive Kingdom of Elmet, Barwick, to the east of Leeds, with the remains of its old castle and fortifications, celebrates its history by preserving a stirring symbol of a pagan past. At over 80 ft, planted in the heart of Main Street, and outstripping even the nearby tower of All Saints church in height, this totem is one of the loftiest maypoles in England.

A forest of poles has sprouted in Barwick down the centuries, but the origins of the triennial hoistings are unclear. One local theory proposes a biblical provenance, suggesting that the Tower of Babel, a symbol of human kind's arrogance, was the original inspiration. Another explanation cites a romantic Roman fable. Kybele, the goddess of flowers and fruitfulness was said to have been fatally gored by a wild boar under a pine tree. Her lover, Attis, believing that the spirit of his maiden had been transferred to the tree, had it felled, transported to Rome and wreathed in garlands and flowers. A focus of mourning, the tree became symbolic of Kybele's resurrection to life, and henceforth poles were associated with rebirth and renewal. Pursuing this theme, other commentators postulate that the maypole rejoices in the re-emergence of spring. Whatever the truth of the matter, Barwick maypole is a year round attraction and a uniquely colourful facet of village life.

Custom dictates that the maypole shall be fashioned from spruce, traditionally supplied free of charge from the lord of the manor's estates at Parlington. Taken down as a precautionary measure every three years, poles would be either discarded or repaired and redecorated. Damaged or infected timber would be removed, new lengths would be spliced in, primed with copper sulphate solution and painted. Well seasoned before use, new poles would also be spliced to attain the desired height.

Surmounted by a tip-top fox, and decorated with candy stripes and splendid garlands made by village ladies (four floribunda displays blossom with 1,500 silk or cotton rosettes, 48 red, white and blue ribbons and 48 bells), the maypole is raised by carefully coordinated and marshalled muscle, 150 Barwick men taking the strain under the overall command of the pole-master. Apart from several stout ropes, a set of multi-height ladders for use as props, and picks and shovels for the hole excavation party (a bucketful of ale is usually donated to the moles by the local landlord), artificial devices or stimulants are strictly taboo.

Barwick's festival and the accompanying carnival are enjoyed by the whole village, and especially by the schoolchildren who supply the maypole queen and her retinue. On floats and tractors, preceded by their queen resplendent in a white dress and blue velvet train, the cavalcade makes its stately way through the village to the strains of a brass band. Arriving in Hall Tower Field, the queen is traditionally crowned by the Lord Mayor, and the enthronement is celebrated by dancing and other entertainments.

Apart from minor alarms and insignificant damage to local buildings as a result of the wobblings of certain rope-men, considering its size and tremendous weight, Barwick maypole has had a remarkably accident-free existence. A sterling testimony to the thoroughness of its erection and implanting, there are no records of collapse, although it has mysteriously disappeared on at least three occasions.

Hardly an opportunistic crime, the first theft occurred in 1829, when the men of Garforth came in the dead of night. The maypole was quickly recovered and almost 80 years elapsed before the next daring snatch, a purloinment of the upper half of the pole by the youth of the fiercely rival village of Aberford. The booty was again reclaimed and the culprits were severely chastised.

The most organised and serious theft of the maypole took place three days before the raising ceremony in 1966. Skulking in the darkness, awaiting Barwick church clock to strike midnight, eight robbers readied their spanners. As the last note drifted across the churchyard, they pounced, dismantling the top section of the maypole and disappearing unobserved; or so they thought. A witness recorded the chilling news . . . 'I live betwixt two not too friendly villages. Also I have a terrier that will follow anything that moves, with tail wagging. On the night of Friday/Saturday, I was awakened by the dog giving teethy growls, barking savagely yet wagging its tail with delight. Now I know the reason for this commotion. The top half of the Barwick maypole was being smuggled past my gate. As the town crier of the maypole raising, I shall never live this down. With the enemy at the gate, I let them pass unchallenged.' Such an admission in former times would have guaranteed a public lynching from what was left of the noble stick, but the good people of Barwick, although angry, had only thoughts of recovery.

The police were called, search parties were despatched and a two seater plane was scrambled to circle the surrounding fields. With the big day looming, it was decided to prepare for the worst, and a trio of lumberjacks were sent east to procure a replacement pole.

Time ebbed away without any hopeful news, and having returned with a substitute length of Swedish pine, carpenters worked all night to save Barwick's pride. Then came dramatic news. Spies who had infiltrated enemy lines, had overheard the boasts of two Aberford boys . . . 'They will never find it where we've put it.' A woodland hunt was on!

The pole was eventually found camouflaged by undergrowth near Parlington Woods. Its discoverer was ecstatic. 'We saw a man standing about a field away and we suspected he was the lookout for the Aberford party. I stayed by the pole and the policeman went back to Barwick to give the alert. Crowds of people returned with him and it turned out to be a really exciting evening.'

Thefts of Barwick's pole have always been speedily remedied, but in 1951, a thousand years of history was threatened by a far more serious fate — the woodsman's axe. An assumed indifference to the plight of the maypole on the part of the pole-masters had led them to sharpen their tools. The felling was arranged for Easter Monday. Rumours spread like wildfire, fanned by a concerned villager who toured the streets acting as a town crier. A public meeting was quickly arranged in the school, and a packed assembly resolved to preserve the maypole at all costs. A committee was elected, money was collected and Barwick's unique heritage was saved.

The joyous maypole adds to the attraction of one of Yorkshire's finest villages. And, on the span of an ancient ley-line, it is also said to exert a magical charm. Wooden slivers are eagerly sought by souvenir hunters, and the pole has long been used in the rite of initiation for newcomers to the village. Only reverent bashing against the pole confers the status of a true Barwicker, and this is a prized identity still.

The Storming of Rawfold's Mill

West Yorkshire's reputation for dour resistance to change is nowhere more violently displayed than in the Luddite riots of 1812. New machines threatened the livelihoods of the handloom weavers and there was an unstoppable call for violence. Incited by Ned Ludd, and alarmed by the activities of William Cartwright, who in 1809 had installed finishing machines in Rawfold's Mill at Cleckheaton, the workers of the Spen valley mobilised for action.

For decades, the economy of the Spen valley had been based on the production of hand made cloth in isolated farmsteads and small workshops. Promising substantial profits for the resourceful entrepreneur, the advent of water powered machinery suddenly cast the shadow of redundancy over the entire workforce, and there were widespread fears of job losses and pauperdom.

The mounting venom of the weavers was directed at Cartwright, who remained resolute in the face of growing intimidation orchestrated by William Hall, a displaced worker himself. Hall and a group of sympathisers organised a series of Saturday night meetings at the Shears Inn, Hightown, Liversedge, hatching a plot to smash the despised machines and swearing on oath never to divulge . . . 'under the canopy of heaven the names of the persons who comprise this secret committee, their proceedings, place of abode, dress, features, complexion or anything else that might lead to the discovery of same, either by word, deed or sign, under the penalty of being sent out of the world by the first brother who shall meet me, and my name and character blotted out of existence and never to be remembered but with contempt and abhorrence.'

Alerted to the delivery of a consignment of machine frames to Rawfold's Mill, the wreckers made their initial attack at night, ambushing the transport waggons at Hartshead. Fearing recognition, the masked Luddites blindfolded and tied the drivers, before wreaking havoc on the frames. Emboldened, they decided to mount an all out attack on the mill on 11th April.

Staggering their departure times to allay suspicions, and armed with a motley collection of guns, hedge stakes, hammers and hatchets, the 150 strong band gathered at midnight to await the arrival of a contingent of accomplices from Leeds. Reinforcements never arrived and a decision was made to storm the mill regardless. Forewarned of the assault, Cartwright and four loyal employees had managed to fortify the mill. Doors and windows were stoutly locked, five armed soldiers took up strategic positions as snipers, and sentries were posted at the mill gates. Unprepared and ill equipped to topple such defence, the Luddites attacked.

Overcoming the sentries, the mob charged the mill,

hurling stones at the windows and firing through the voids. A knot of men attempted to break down the barricaded door, but under the withering musket fire of the defenders they were forced to retreat, finally calling off the action as they quickly ran out of ammunition and resolve.

Two of the Luddites were critically wounded and once the firing had stopped agonised cries echoed in the yard. 'For God's sake shoot me and put me out of my misery,' implored the 24 year old Samuel Hartley who was dragged away by his comrades. Taken, together with the bullet-raked John Booth to the Old Yew Tree Inn, and then on to the Star Inn in Roberttown, Hartley died. The 19 year old Booth expired soon afterwards. Bravely, neither man betrayed the cause.

News of the attack spread throughout Yorkshire and beyond. Surviving a further attempt on his life, the victorious Cartwright became a national celebrity, although in the Spen valley he was regarded with contempt and loathing. Cartwright offered evidence which lead to the arrest of William Hall and 16 of his followers, and with obscene alacrity, the accused were tried, convicted and publicly hanged with the words of Judge Baron Thompson ringing in their ears. 'It is of infinite importance to society that no mercy should be shown to you. It is important that your sentence should be speedily carried out and it is but right to tell you that you have but a very short time to remain in this world. I trust not only those who now hear me but all without these walls to whom the tiding of your fate may come, will be warned by your fate.'

There was a grisly sequel to the storming of

Rawfold's Mill. During the attack, a defending soldier had conscientiously refused to fire on 'his brothers'. Sentenced after a court martial to 300 strokes of the cat o' nine tails, the prisoner was led to Primrose Lane near the scene of his offence. Bound to a stake and ringed by a detachment of Redcoats armed with muskets and fixed bayonets, the man was stripped and the punishment began. Horrified, but helpless and unable to interfere, the crowd gasped at each bloody stroke. Cries for mercy went unheeded as the remorseless flagellation pulped flesh exposed like a side of raw meat. At last, the pleas of William Cartwright, who had originally reported the unfortunate soldier for dereliction of duty, were heard, and the lashing ceased. Thus ended one of the most unsavoury chapters in West Yorkshire's history.

A Brontë Childhood

Only four miles from Keighley, at an elevation of 800 ft, Haworth during the 19th century was a remote and an insular town, where attitudes to strangers matched the inhospitability of the surrounding hills.

The Brontë family — the Reverend Patrick, his sickly wife Maria and six children, made the uncomfortable journey to Haworth in 1820. Arriving in a procession of seven carts, struggling on the flag-stoned ascent with the stench of open privies in their nostrils, they climbed to the parsonage. Solidly built to withstand the northern gales, cramped and austerely furnished, and as a precaution against fire, bereft of carpets and curtains, it stood cold and aloof only yards from the sombre parish church. A temple of literary invention, this was to be the home of the Brontë children in their formative years.

Not surprisingly, the newcomers received a bluff welcome from inhabitants described as wild and fiercely independent, and there seems to have been little integration other than through the church. Absorbed in their own disciplined life, dictated by a stern and a largely absent father who was preoccupied with his ministry and in the comforting of his poorly wife, the 'wild eyed' children spent much time indoors reading and entertaining themselves, gravitating, when the weather was kind, to the purpled moors. Nourished by the plainest of food, stunted and shabbily dressed by fatherly decree — deploring any apparel which did not have a purely utilitarian purpose, he once threw on the fire several pairs of little coloured boots donated by a friend — Maria, Elizabeth, Charlotte, Patrick Branwell, Emily Jane and Anne, frequently explored the boundless sea of heather and gorse.

But the carefree days of infancy were short lived. Little more than a year after moving to Haworth, the children's mother died of cancer. A double tragedy followed. Maria, who Patrick Brontë regarded as the brightest of his daughters, contracted tuberculosis and died slowly in 1825. Similarly afflicted, Elizabeth expired one month later. At the tender age of eight, Charlotte found herself the matron of the house.

For five long years, the children were closeted in Haworth, with little contact with an outside world locally prone to typhoid and other serious diseases. Taught by their father and by an aunt, they studied the classics and they were allowed to read popular magazines and to discuss current affairs with the whole family. Weekly music lessons under the tutelage of the church organist were arranged, the services of a drawing master from Leeds were engaged and the children were encouraged to keep a succession of pets, although contact with other children was generally denied and there was a noticeable sparsity of toys. Cocooned, their natural boisterousness and zest for games inhibited by disciplined isolation, the children escaped into unhealthy realms of fantasy, the 'infernal world', or the 'place beneath' vying with play writing for popularity.

The children conjured up fantastic tales, some inspired by a rare box of wooden toys brought back by Patrick Brontë after a visit to Leeds. Scribbling down the plots on scraps of paper, properly sewn along the spines to form miniature booklets and magazines, the budding authors created extraordinary kingdoms — Verdopolis, Gondal and Angria — inhabited by heroes and demons. There were passionate and satanic relationships, wars, murders and torrid accounts of love. Beguiled, mesmerised by chimeras of their own invention, the children were swept along in a tide of ever wilder imaginings, using their secret games as mental bolt-holes. What should have been mere diversions, became morbid escapes from normality. Recognising the dangers, the Brontë girls managed to disentangle themselves and to find more wholesome pursuits. But Branwell was forever smitten.

The smouldering seeds of expression sown during these early days of literary adventure would later blossom in such controversial and tempestuous works as *Jane Eyre, Wuthering Heights, Agnes Grey, The Tenant of Wildfell Hall, Shirley* and *Villette*. The girls all achieved varying degrees of literary fame. But what of Branwell? Despite his obvious talent and early promise, in the shadow of his sisters he became a waster, a frequenter of Haworth's Black Bull and an opium addict, a black thorn amidst the bloom of genius.

In any century, in any culture, given the

wherewithal to scribe, the Brontë sisters would have produced competent prose. Strange then that the Fates should conspire a 19th century childhood in cheerless yet inspirational Haworth?

The Wise Woman of Wakefield

Jennet Benton had all the attributes of a witch. A stooped-backed, wizened old crone with a baleful eye and a dutiful cat, she lived in the town of Wakefield in the 17th century, and was widely known amongst its inhabitants for her potions and wise ways.

Jennet shared her humble mud-walled cottage with her son, George Benton, a former Roundhead soldier, a loafer and frequenter of taverns who lived on the dubious earnings of his mother. Renowned for her love philtres, Jennet was widely consulted on affairs of the heart. She also had a reputation as a fortune teller and as a divine, being particularly valued by local farmers in predicting the most propitious times for sowing and reaping. The idea that this oracle was a witch, and had regular intercourse with the Devil, was widely prevalent in the district, but such was Jennet's undoubted value to the community, that all suggestions that she be subjected to the test for witchcraft were ignored.

Over the years, however, the notion that Jennet was in league with dark forces took deeper root. Her feline companion was a monstrous black beast, which generally responded to visitors by arching its back and spitting. On one occasion, however, a handsome

young man visited the cottage, and the cat was seen to purr and to rub up against the gentleman with obvious affection. Observers said that the visitor was really the Devil in disguise. By way of further indictment, Jennet's regular absences from the cottage were explained as attendances at witches' sabbaths. The temporary disappearances of her broom from its usual place in the doorway were regarded as additional proof.

Toleration of Jennet's arcane craft continued, but then the action of a neighbour, Richard Jackson, who owned Bunny Hall Farm near her cottage, led to a dispute, the consequences of which were to have diabolical effects.

Public use of a disputed right-of-way across the farmland had increasingly led to crop damage, and the farmer, determined to prevent further losses, blocked the path. Local people were outraged, and, led by Jennet and her son, they defied the obstruction.

Mounting the locked gate, Jennet and her son were one day confronted by Jackson's bailiff, who in an altercation received injuries to his face. Immediately, Jackson instituted legal proceedings for trespass and assault, the guilty verdict inciting Jennet to action.

Shortly after his court appearance, Jackson called at his neighbour's cottage in conciliatory mood. Jennet was at the door heating a cauldron of herbs with the bristling cat at her side.

'Ah, Mother Benton, busy as usual I see, preparing something for the benefit of one of your clients.'

'It is no business of yours what I am preparing. I sent not for you, nor do I want your conversation or interference in my concerns. Go your way, or it may be the worse for you.'

'Nay, good dame, be not angry. I came not to interfere with your concerns; I merely stopped on my road home to say "good even" to you, and to see if I could be of any service to you, for I desire to cultivate the good will of my neighbours.'

'And a pretty way of doing so by prosecuting them in law courts for maintaining the rights of themselves and their ancestors for generations past.'

'That I was compelled to do, good Jennet, for the maintenance of my own rights. It was a necessity forced upon me, but I bear no ill-will to either you or your son. And see, as a proof thereof, I have brought you a new kirtle from Wakefield.' He threw the garment on her lap.

Inflamed, Jennet tore up the gift and tossed it into the fire with the imprecation, 'I will listen no more to your hypocritical palaver . . . soon you shall know what it is to incur the wrath of Jennet Benton, the wise woman of Wakefield. Within a twelvemonth and a day, Farmer Jackson, shall you find at what cost you set the myrmidons of the law upon me and my belongings, and from that time to your life's end shall you rue that day's work. It is I, the wise woman of Wakefield, who say it, and see if I am not a good soothsayer. . . .'

A level headed farmer, not given to fanciful superstition, Jackson had previously ignored Jennet's rantings, but there began a series of bizarre happenings which convinced even he that mischief was afoot.

Bunny Hall Farm became haunted. Furniture was moved by invisible hands. Utensils were flung about the room and more terrifying still, Jackson's wife was inexplicably struck deaf.

And the catalogue of sorrows continued. One of Jackson's children developed epilepsy, a herd of pigs smashed through two barn doors and bolted, and Jackson himself experienced strange fits, hearing the hypnotic sound of music and dancing accompanied by pealing bells. At first, Jackson regarded his ordeal as an hallucination. Then other people heard the noises and all were convinced of Jennet's curse, calling for the immediate execution of the ultimate test for witchcraft.

This quaint ritual entailed stripping the accused, tying her thumbs to her big toes and casting her into a deep pond. If the victim drowned, brutal logic decreed that she was indisputably innocent. If she floated, the verdict was guilty and she was purified at the stake!

A sensible and humane man despite his torment, Jackson decided against barbarism and opted for the justice of the courts. Jennet Benton and her son George were sent for trial at York Assizes on 7th June 1656.

Arraigned before Justice Ward, the accused heard evidence from Jackson and two other witnesses of 'apparitions like black dogges and cats . . . jumping up the chimney over the hot coals', of fleeing servants, of slamming doors, demoniacal laughter, agonised shrieks, flapping bats' wings and the general sickliness of the household. With great firmness, Jennet accepted that she had cursed Jackson, 'It is true I called down the wrath of Heaven upon him . . .' but she strenuously denied the charges and was surprisingly acquitted.

But was she a witch, and did that most articulate of lawyers have a satanic word in the good judge's ear?

Yorkshire Pennies

The old town of Pontefract with its liquorice cakes, or 'Yorkshire pennies', is famous throughout the land. But why was Pontefract so lusciously blessed? According to legend, the answer is strange indeed.

The sweet root of the mauve flowering pea has long been invested with magical and medicinal properties. The Egyptians believed that liquorice could ward off evil spirits, whilst the Chinese, as early as 3000 BC, supposed that it could prolong life and endow strength. Well known in the ancient world, liquorice only appeared in Yorkshire in the current millenium, its introduction being attributed by some to a Pontefract schoolmaster.

Enjoying a coastal holiday at the time of the Spanish Armada, the gentleman is said to have picked up a bunch of sticks recently washed ashore from a sunken galleon. A true Tyke with an eye for a providential bargain, this rod-wielding disciplinarian wondered if the sticks might be a substitute for the cane, and he was anxious to try them out on his return to Yorkshire. The floggings were a great success, so much so that the unfortunate pupils resorted to biting on shreds of the liquorice to stifle their cries. Strangely, the beatings became popular, the masochistic tendencies of Pontefract schoolboys denied all but the meanest confections eventually being explained by the pleasant tasting liquorice, whose anaesthetic qualities helped dull the pain. Swept into the school garden, pieces of the plant gradually took root, giving rise to an industry that flourished for 400 years. And to this day, the term coined by the miscreants of long ago is still in use. Do you remember asking for 'Spanish'?

This fanciful account of Pontefract's connection with liquorice, it has to be said, is not borne out by historical facts. It is reasonable to assume, however, that the cultivation of the plant was promoted in Pontefract by the Cluniac order of monks as early as the 11th century. Used as a mouth deodorant and for medicinal purposes, liquorice was prescribed by the eminent Greek physician Theophrastus for asthma and dry cough and in general troubles of the chest. 'It is also administered in honey for wounds. It has the property of quenching thirsts . . . wherefore they say that the Scythians, with this and mare's milk cheese can go for eleven or twelve days without drinking.'

Under monastic husbandry, and in the shadow of the greatest fortress in Europe, the plant continued to be grown for its curative effects, being particularly beneficial in the alleviation of chest and stomach complaints, but it was not until 1760, when an enterprising local chemist George Dunhill added sugar to the original recipe, that the modern sweetmeat was born. The eventual demand for Yorkshire pennies can be judged by the output of nimble fingered ladies who were expected to shape and stamp up to 25,000 cakes in a single eight hour day!

Liquorice grew well in Pontefract because of the

deep fertile loam and mild climate of the Friarwood valley. But contrary to popular belief, growing conditions were not unique to the town, and in 1701 the borough council enacted a local by-law prohibiting the sale of buds and sets to people living outside the district. Cultivation reached its peak in the late 18th and early 19th centuries and then declined rapidly after the war with the importation of cheaper supplies from Mediterranean countries. Although specimen liquorice plants survive in Pontefract's parks and gardens, the last commercial crop was harvested in 1966, the vestiges of cultivation finally withering in a Bondgate field in 1972.

Yet the legacy of Yorkshire pennies and a host of other novelty sweets — coils, pipes and liquorice allsorts — lives on. And there hangs another remarkable, and this time, an irrefutably accurate, tale.

A mistake by a tipsy salesman created liquorice allsorts. Charlie Thompson, who was employed by the Sheffield firm of Bassetts, hopelessly mixed up his customer samples after an inebriate party. Quick witted despite the drink, Charlie passed off the sweets as a new line, launching his liquorice allsorts to an eager trade. Sales rocketed, Pontefract firms responding to the astonishing demand by producing their own lines.

Satisfying a niche demand in a confectionery market now worth hundreds of millions of pounds per year, Pontefract's liquorice manufacture flourishes under the able management of local firm Wilkinson's. In the 3,000 years since Tutankhamun's gilded tomb was provisioned with its own supplies of liquorice, tastes have come full circle. Today, the magical health properties of liquorice are again being promoted by specialist shops. Yorkshire children chew on regardless. Like Egyptian royalty, they have always known that Yorkshire pennies were as good as gold.

Prophet Wroe

John Wroe, the self styled Yorkshire Moses, was born in Bowling near Bradford in 1792. A poor scholar, and an indifferent businessman, 'Pudding Wroe', so called from his habit of asking for 'Nowt but pudding' after arising from one of his famous trances, was nevertheless a persuasive orator who fooled thousands.

After the failure of his wool-combing business in 1819, John Wroe became ill. He was expected to die of fever, but he made a modest recovery, seeking solace in his Bible. He roamed the countryside, reciting scripture and falling into prolonged epileptic fits, alleging trances and consort with spirits. On 12th November 1819, whilst walking in the fields, he reported contact with a vision . . . 'A woman came to me, and tossed me up and down in the field. I endeavoured to lay hold of her, but could not; I therefore knew it was a spirit.'

There followed a series of epileptic fits. John Wroe was struck blind, regaining his sight in the miraculous laying on of hands foretold in the visitation of an angel. After seeking divine guidance in choosing a sect which could best use his talents, the letters 'A. A.

Rabbi, Rabbi, Rabbi' appeared on the tester of his bedstead, and a ministry to the Jews was begun by visiting synagogues in Yorkshire and elsewhere.

Energised by his large following, and convinced of his own apostolic power, John Wroe, in February 1824, announced his intention to walk on water! He was to be baptised in the river Aire near Idle Thorpe and 'glory making sunbeams were to illuminate his head'. A crowd of some 30,000 eager spectators gathered to see the show. The 'hero of light' arrived on an ass, and every available vantage point was secured by craning necks, anxious not to miss the promised miracle. Delayed by clouds, the immersion was postponed, but the multitude, deciding that the prophet had lost his nerve, shouted 'He dussn't go in! He's runnin' away!' Persuaded to dip a toe, Wroe moved forward. The band struck up and the crowd jeered. 'Drown him!' was the cry. The spectacle ended in pandemonium. There was no imitation of Christ's Galilean stroll and the bystanders went berserk, pelting Wroe and his followers with stones and sods.

Later that year, Wroe was publicly circumcised. In answer to a celestial call, there followed a period of wandering in the wilderness. Living on nuts, wheat, blackberries, hips, herbs and water, Wroe again had divine commands, reporting to his wife that he had been instructed to 'destroy all pictures, portraits, or likenesses of anything he had created or caused to grow, whether of iron, stone, wood, cloth, or paper, and everything of a black colour that could be found within the house.'

Eventually, Wroe was acknowledged as the leader of the Southcottian movement in the district. (The founder of the sect, Joanna Southcott, declared that she was to have been the mother of Shiloh, and was to live for ever!) Flaunting his position as 'Prophet of the Lord', Wroe announced that the Lord had decreed that seven virgins were to be sent to comfort and cherish him. Several followers obliged amidst much scandal.

In 1831, Wroe revealed a vocation to depart on a mission. His acolytes raised a considerable sum of money for expenses, and the prophet departed for 14 days. Becoming suspicious, certain followers decided to investigate Wroe's absence. Following his wife, they were led to a cornfield, where they witnessed a sybaritic feast. Incensed at the subterfuge, the spies arrested Wroe, tied him up and led him on a donkey to Pudsey, where he was thrown repeatedly into a pond.

Despite his flagrant dishonesty, Wroe was still revered by many of his supporters and he continued his evil ways. Seeking to raise money, he announced that the Lord had decided that every member of the House of Israel was to purchase a gold ring valued at £1 3s 6d. Wroe provided about 6,000 rings to the members of his organisation and it was not until a wary recipient tested his purchase with nitric acid, that another misdemeanour was revealed.

Wroe's greatest deceit was in the erection of the 'House of Israel'. Commanded by the Lord to build a mansion, he launched a fund, deciding that even the poorest of his followers were to contribute at least ten per cent of their earnings. During 1855 and 1856, Post Office orders were sent in large numbers to Wrenthorpe in Wakefield, where the mansion was to be built. It was said at the time that the subscriptions received amounted to more than the trade income for the entire town. Having secured adequate funds, land was bought in Wrenthorpe, together with upwards of 100 acres of additional pasturage. Incredibly, the property was conveyed to Wroe, and dedicated in a will to his offspring.

Like Southcott, Wroe had promised his followers that he would never die. Some were surprised at his demise in 1862, but others just scoffed at yet another false prophet.

The Bradford Chimney Disaster

Totems of West Yorkshire industrialists, rearing up amongst the mean hovels of the mill workers, factory chimneys have always cast a shadow of oppression over those who toiled in their midst. And the factory chimney in the industrial complex known as Ripley's Mills in Bradford, was more oppressive than most.

A 255 ft octagonal dragon, embellished with ornamental panels and a heavy cornice which consumed three bargeloads of stone alone, it was erected in 1863 on the instructions of Henry William Ripley. The site chosen for the monster was, incredibly, on abandoned coal workings, whose voids were rammed with stone and masked with concrete, to allow building to begin on uneven foundations.

Construction was slow and problematic. At a height of 70 ft, contractors John Moulson and Sons discovered that the chimney was out of plumb. An expert proposed replacing a stringing course on the canted side with slightly smaller bricks. The repair was effected, damaging some of the five ft long throughs linking the inner and outer casing, and the chimney was raised to full height. Only three years elapsed before further repairs were required.

Serving a number of industrial premises including worsted spinners and a wool-top makers, the chimney soon became an object of foreboding. Local residents claimed to have seen the structure sway, cracks appeared, fragments of masonry fell to the ground and starlings nested in the fissures, much to the chagrin of chief stoker Samuel Oddy. 'They used to whistle at us. We often thought it was the masters whistling, and when we stopped and looked round they'd whistle again.'

On 20th December 1882, a visitor to the mill yard inspected the chimney and to his horror noticed a distortion of the brickwork on the south-eastern side. An urgent but superficial survey revealed that the inner and outer casings were becoming detached, and an immediate repair was ordered.

The remedial work was regarded as routine maintenance, and apart from cordoning off the area and stationing a look-out to warn workers of the danger of falling stones, precautions were not thought necessary. Work continued over the annual Christmas holiday, a period of exceptionally wet and windy weather, and was still ongoing when the boilers were relit on 27th December. That portentous day, substantial amounts of stone fell from the chimney damaging the scaffolding, and a violent storm in the night caused one resident of the area to remark, 'Mother, the wind is strong; I would not care if yon chimney were to fall before I go.'

Innocents Day, Thursday 28th December 1882, began in sombre mood, 13 year old apprentice James Hancock expressing the fear of many child workers in his appeal to his widowed mother. 'Don't let me go this morning; somebody will be killed at that place before break time.' 'It's my rent week,' explained his mother, 'you must go.'

Three or four tons of stone dropped from the chimney around eight o'clock. The noise of the crash was drowned by the hum of machinery and there was little panic. During the customary stoppage for breakfast, workers relaxed and drank tea whilst staff members read the morning newspapers. Then the world caved in.

At ten minutes past eight, the chimney suffered a catastrophic failure and collapsed, dropping its fatal debris on the factories below. The storeyed premises tumbled like a house of cards.

Alerted by the rupturing of his furnaces, Samuel Oddy managed to dash out into the yard and pull a visiting carter to safety, and hearing the roar of destruction, several children succeeded in diving for cover. The speed of the collapse, however, prevented the raising of a general alarm, and scores of workers were buried under mountains of rubble.

The settling dust revealed a scene of total devastation, haunted by the screams of the trapped and dying. Frantic and unbelieving, the rescuers who first arrived clawed with their bare hands at the smoking, tangled ruins, risking their own lives in brave attempts at extricating the survivors. With heroic efforts, factory overlooker Tom Nicholl lowered himself precariously by a strap onto a teetering third floor building. With the aid of ladders, he plucked a huddle of frightened boys and girls to safety, as other rescuers, guided by cries for help, burrowed to aid those who had miraculously escaped death.

The civic response to the tragedy was reported to have been muted, the Lord Mayor sending his condolences, a case of eau de Cologne and several bunches of grapes to the Infirmary, where large crowds had gathered to watch the procession of casualties.

At Ripley's Mills, the search for survivors gradually became more organised. Two hundred and eighty volunteers, split into two shifts, worked under arc lights where necessary to free the entombed. A succession of corpses were carried to a makeshift mortuary in a nearby warehouse, and the grisly work continued, hour after hour.

When all hope was fading of finding further survivors, a ten year old boy, trapped for 36 hours, was dragged from the rubble. The euphoria lasted only briefly as the body count commenced, the authorities allowing sightseers to file past the debris and to deposit their relief fund coins in collecting sheets.

In excess of 70 people were injured and 54 died in the calamity. Draped in sacking, some mutilated beyond recognition, the bodies were lined up for the inspection of grieving relatives. Paid for by the Ripley family, funerals were quickly arranged, the services being all the more poignant because of the tender age of some of the deceased.

An immediate consequence of the disaster was a heightening of public awareness of the inherent dangers of poorly built chimneys. The tragedy at Ripley's Mills had been well publicised, and people in West Yorkshire and elsewhere became vociferous in demanding higher constructional standards and regular safety checks.

In a mood of public disquiet, the coroner's inquest and inquiry opened on 29th December in Bradford Town Hall. For a month the jury examined the evidence, listening to first hand accounts from experts and workers alike, of the factors likely to have contributed to the disaster. The verdict was as follows:

> 'We find that the owners did all that non-practical men could reasonably be expected to do under the circumstances, and therefore we do not attach any blame to them, or find them guilty of negligence; and give as our verdict "Accidental death". We are of the opinion that the foundation was good, and that the fall of the chimney was partly due to the cutting, aided by the strong wind on the morning of the accident, and regret the works were not stopped during the repairs.'

For all who had been heartily disturbed by this most avoidable of tragedies, the comment of *The Globe* was answer enough. 'A more unsatisfactory finding has rarely been arrived at in a court of law.'

School Days
at Ackworth

Founded in 1779, Ackworth School has always coddled its charges, as a key-hole squint down the years shows. Inspired by the principles of Quakerism, the academy was established by Dr John Fothergill as a bold philanthropic experiment aimed at creating an educational community for the children of less affluent parents.

Pupils were recruited from all over England, many travelling great distances, sometimes on foot, to begin a regimented life in the wilds of Yorkshire.

Boys and girls were strictly segregated, and were dressed according to precise rules . . . 'the cocked hat, the long-tailed coat, the leather breeches, and the buckled shoe, were the dress even of boys; the girls figure in white caps, the hair turned back under them or combed straight down upon the forehead, checked aprons with bibs, and white neck handkerchiefs, folded neatly over their stuff gowns in front.'

Rising at six o'clock in summer, and at seven o'clock in the colder months, children were expected to lead exemplary lives devoted to study, prayer and decorum, and the consequences of misdemeanour were dire. Punishment consisted of confiscation of 'spice' (the weekly allowance for sweetmeats was one penny), 'disgracing' and corporal punishment. Culprits, often with their hands tied, were 'disgraced' by frog marching, or they were made to stand to attention for hours in public places, these particular humiliations being subsequently deepened by the compulsory displaying of hand-held boards listing the crimes for all to see. Canings, whippings and floggings for more heinous offences were later supplemented by the introduction of solitary confinement.

However, compared to the inmates of other establishments, the Ackworth pupils were a pampered lot, and although they were subjected to a rigorous regime, they were generally happy, healthy and stoutly fed, as a typical menu shows.

BILL OF FARE
Breakfast
Milk porridge poured on bread.

Dinner
First day: Boil'd suet puddings with currants: sometimes apple pies; in summer occasionally other fruit pies or cheese-cakes.
Second day: Beef or mutton, dressed by steam, with potatoes or greens and bread. No butter.
Third day: Meat soup. In summer this dinner may be occasionally changed for bacon with beans, peas, lettuces or other roots or greens and bread. No butter.
Fourth day: Boil'd suet pudding with sweet sauce.
Fifth day: Baked batter puddings with sweet sauce. Sometimes baked rice puddings.

Sixth day: Beef or mutton dressed by steam (sometimes a little pork) with turnips, carrots, greens or potatoes and bread. No butter.
Seventh day: Meat soup.

Supper
Bread and cheese and beer on First Days. Butter instead of cheese when butter is plentiful.
All the rest of the week milk and bread. Two ounces of butter is considered a proper allowance for each child: the butter to be spread on the bread for them.

Beer and water for drink; except First Days, then to have beer at supper.

Although breakfasts were popular, the suet puddings, or 'Solid Lumps' as they were more commonly known, were universally disliked, and the batter pudding or 'Clatty Vengeance' was dreaded! Regaled with such a cornucopia of delights, diners possessed a remarkable sense of humour, as was demonstrated by a boy who discovered a fully feathered cock's head in his soup and chirped 'Cock-a-doodle-do' to his chums. Not that the victuals were all bad. What boarder today would dream of being sent to bed with a tummy full of ale?

But students had to sing for their suppers. Apart from studying English language, writing and arithmetic (and housewifery and needlework for the girls), they were also expected to share in the domestic and manual duties of the household and farm. Boys were asked to wait at table, clean shoes and knives, to help in the bakery, dairy and garden, and on the farm, whilst girls were encouraged to mend linen, act as serving maids at the Householder's table, and assist the laundress and the mantua maker.

School days were long and there was little time for play, an occupation severely restricted by rules prohibiting raucous games and the use of kites and other playthings. The children, however, improvised and devised a whole range of pastimes, including an incredible game of leapfrog, sometimes involving 180 raised bottoms in one long line! Skipping was also popular, and in winter, gleefully treading down the snow, whole gaggles of boys would prepare a rink of ice, using skates made from narrow strips of wood to cavort with Ackworth's shoemaker, a compulsive skater dressed in his dapper Quaker costume and broad brimmed beaver hat.

Having taken a measured peep at Ackworth school life, it is fair to say that it was a reasonably enjoyable experience, although this enjoyment was, for some, soured by a daily regime that has terrorised boys and girls since the dawn of time. Ablutions boy! To the sink girl! Ackworth's clarion calls to wash were the rudest of awakenings.

Roused cringing, the children were led to an icy confrontation with a water filled trough in the cellar. Obligatory gargling followed. This daily routine was complemented in summer by a route march visitation to the infamous 'Bath', a walled, perennially chilled chalybeate pool half a mile from the school. Veiled in a repulsive yellow scum, the bath was said to have had therapeutic properties, and boys were encouraged to strip naked and fearlessly take the plunge. Girls, with an acknowledgement to decency, were allowed to wear cast-off, often oversize dresses as makeshift bathing costumes, and, whereas the boys were expected to dress without drying, girls were afforded the luxury of two roller towels between the entire company. The efficacy of these immersions was judged by the lack of fatalities! After their soak, pupils were rewarded with a piece of bread.

In later years of the academy, which flourishes still, the students were further spoiled with heated classrooms, electric lighting and piped water. But progress was not always for the best. The beer ration was dispensed with years ago, and wine gums are a poor substitute.

The Coal Dust Knight

Miners throughout the world have cause to be thankful for the pioneering work of Sir William Edward Garforth. A zealous and much admired local politician and manager of the Silkstone Pit in Altofts near Wakefield, Garforth is best remembered for breaking windows! Such were the pyrotechnical consequences of his exhaustive experiments into the dangers of coal dust, that the village school was often closed. The children recalled their school days with affection!

Of Yorkshire stock, Garforth was born in Cheshire on 30th December 1845. Industry was in his blood, his grandfather having founded the Dukenfield Iron Works in 1825. Interested in a career in mining, he trained as an engineer, leaving his home in 1879 to take up the post of agent to what was then Pope and Pearson's Colliery in Altofts.

Displaying great energy and a genuine vocation for political service, the newcomer was quickly elected to the Local Board, an institution he served with verve and dedication for many years. But his pre-eminent talent was as a mining pioneer, and, in 1882, his proposals for tackling a problem that had vexed the industry for years, set him on a course of discovery and invention that was to lead to international fame.

73

Volatile and highly combustible impurities in coal, exported from his own pit to the USA, had ignited in transit, causing devastating shipboard fires. Addressing a Board of Trade Inquiry, Garforth recommended that all future shipments should be washed and screened to reduce the risk of explosion. In subsequent trials his ideas were proved to work and his prestige grew.

Altofts, as with other mining communities, experienced the perennial problems of low pay, atrocious working conditions and social hardship, but Garforth was an ameliorating and a benevolent force, working tirelessly, both publicly and professionally, to improve village life. Then, in what was recognised as 'one of the best managed collieries in England', at three o'clock in the afternoon of Saturday, 2nd October 1886, there was a terrible explosion and fire underground.

The clearing smoke and fumes revealed a scene of utter carnage — the charred and mangled flesh of 21 men and 53 horses — the ultimate nightmare in mining. Quickly on the scene, Garforth organised the rescue of survivors, deploying the Rescue Corps, a body he had set up shortly after his arrival in Yorkshire. Entering the mine himself with a crew of deputies in an attempt to locate the source of the explosion and to confront the still raging blaze, he crawled for hours on his hands and knees in appalling conditions, constantly noting, assessing and planning for the recovery of the mine. His subsequent publication *Rules for Recovering Coal Mines After Explosions and Fires* became a standard text book.

Appalled at the tragic loss of life, Garforth's passion

for improvements in mine safety knew no bounds, and his experimentations took on a new vigour. Mad professor jokes had a popular appeal in Silkstone Row and adjacent mining properties, and residents learned to tolerate the occasional explosions and lost panes, being generously rewarded for their forbearance by annual presentations of Christmas turkeys!

After a battery of exhaustive tests a number of complementary improvements were made. Traditionally, the threat of coal dust explosion in mines had been countered by spraying. Garforth proved that the application of stone dust was more effective. He introduced modern miners' lamps and installed electric lighting, replacing the primitive furnace used for ventilation with a fan. Another significant advance was the phasing out of blasting powder. This was replaced by dynamite, an infinitely more stable explosive. Longer term, he perfected a gas-testing device and breathing apparatus dubbed the 'Weg' after his own initials. So pleased were the mine directors at the performance of their manager, that in June 1887 he was rewarded with a formal dinner and gift presentation at the Station Hotel in Normanton, Mr Richard Pope presenting a silver token 'as a small mark of the untiring energy and self-sacrificing devotion displayed in the work of exploration and recovery and subsequently of the restoration of the pit.'

In 1893, reduced wages caused grievous suffering in the Yorkshire coalfield. The inevitable withdrawal of labour only exacerbated the situation. There were riots and disturbances quelled by armed troops and real fears of starvation in Altofts and elsewhere. A uniquely compassionate man, a singularly trusted and respected representative of the colliery owning classes, Garforth stood alone amongst his kind, a warm hearted intermediary, providing daily breakfasts for miners' children in Altofts Colliery School, and writing to the miners' leaders of his concerns . . . 'I am anxious that no unnecessary friction should be caused in this village . . . considering the amicable way we have worked together for so many years.'

In bad times and good, Garforth continued to work for his constituents and to refine his inventions and techniques. He lectured widely, he was visited by mining professionals and students from around the world, and in 1908 he was presented to King Edward VII. A succession of honours acknowledged his great work. He was elected President of the Institute of Mining Engineers, and in 1912 he was presented for the degree of Doctor of Laws at the University of Birmingham, the presentation speech summing up an outstanding career. 'As an engineer, his energy and ability have been vigorously devoted to the progress of mining science. By his efforts in the systematic application of scientific principles to coal mining he has rendered high service to the country and has done much to further the safe working of mines.' The crowning approbation was a knighthood. In 1914, Altofts doffed its cap to Sir William Edward Garforth.

Garforth died on the 1st October 1921 leaving an eternal legacy. Following his lead, mine rescue stations were established all over the globe. Whenever the black dust sparks he is remembered.

Denby Dale Whoppers

The citizens of Denby Dale are known the world over for their enormous pies. The inaugural crust was baked in 1788 to commemorate the returning to sanity of King George III. Since then there has been a succession of whoppers.

The next communal madness was inspired by the Duke of Wellington's victory at Waterloo, the 1815 pie consisting of two sheep, 20 fowl and half a peck of flour cooked in a local kiln.

Almost a generation passed before a third pie was baked to mark the repealing of the Corn Laws. Noah's Ark had less meat than this monster, which consumed 44½ stones of flour, nine and a half lbs of lard, 16lbs of butter, one calf, 100 lbs of beef, five sheep, two ducks, two geese, two turkeys, two guinea fowl, four hens, six pigeons, 63 small birds, seven hares, 14 rabbits, four grouse, four pheasants and four partridges!

When cooked, the pie was hauled by 13 horses to the dismembering ground, superstitions about the unlucky number of nags, swamped in a melee of hungry mouths. The 15,000 strong crowd clamoured to be served, jostling and pushing until the platform collapsed, flinging the pie to the winds, its contents

being devoured in a state of turmoil and wild confusion.

Bad luck again dogged the fourth extravaganza — the professionally baked Queen Victoria Jubilee pie of August 1887. An excess of game was used and hot and cold ingredients were fatally blended in a salmonellic stew, instantly condemned and given a ceremonial burial in a local wood. A poetical adieu composed as the chef beat a hasty retreat to London said it all:—

In Affectionate Remembrance of the
Denby Dale Pie
which died August 27th 1887
Aged three days
And was interred in Quick Lime with much rejoicing
in
Toby Wood. Sunday August 28th 1887
With the Committee's regrets.
'Strong, strong was the smell that compelled us to part.
From a treat to our stomach and a salve to our heart:
Like the last Denby Pie which the crowd did assail.
Its contents a rank mixture it quickly turned stale.
Though we could not eat, yet we lingered near.
Till the stench proved too much for our nasals to bear:
So like sensible men the committee did say.
Twas best to inter it without further delay.'

Undaunted, the determined mourners fashioned a second pie almost before its predecessor had gone cold. The 'Resurrection Pie', this time entrusted to experienced amateur cooks, was a complete success.

Triggered, perhaps, by lunar or planetary cycles, pie mania normally strikes every 20–30 years. The

79

sixth monster, appearing in 1896, was therefore an aberration, baked ostensibly to celebrate the jubilee of the repeal of the Corn Laws, although a local resident suggested that 'when people have felt like baking a pie, they have made one and found the excuse afterwards.' In its half ton dish specially made by W. C. Holmes of Huddersfield, this pie was serenaded by brass bands, another memorable Denby Dale occasion ending with a splendid firework display.

Enter pie number seven, the 1928 'Infirmary Pie' conceived as a belated beano saluting the end of the First World War, with the added purpose of raising £1,000 for the District Hospital. Anxious to avoid a repetition of the 1887 debacle, the recipe expressly excluded game. Despite this, the old problems recurred and four barrowloads of offending meat had to be surreptitiously abandoned before the ceremonials could begin. In a huge dish, the pie was mounted on wheels so that cooking could be strictly controlled. Thirty hours later, the crust, whose dough had been rolled in the Salvation Army Hall in sections, was ready for the knife, but like a reluctant baby, the pie refused to budge. It would not leave the oven. Coaxing with crow-bars proved useless, so lengths of tram-lines and jacks were requisitioned, the hour long puffing and heaving of 20 men finally succeeding in moving the four ton goliath onto an awaiting wagon. This promptly began to sink! Once more into the breach the gallant brawn of Denby Dale persevered, and at long last the pie was delivered and enjoyed by over 100,000 visitors.

Four royal births prompted the 1964 bash. The giant pie dish was launched as a ship, the 'Denby Dale', crewed on the nearby canal by pretty girls, VIPs and various representatives of the media. Gobbling two stones of baking powder alone, the pie raised money for the erection of a community centre — the Pie Hall — the 18 ft long dish ending its days as a flower bed.

Financial realities shaped the 1988 'Bicentenary Pie', whose fortunes were assigned to the Denby Dale Pie Trust (a newly registered charity) and a Leeds firm of promotion and sponsorship consultants. Conformation with the all important health and hygiene regulations was the responsibility of the 170 strong Technical Committee, a stalwart band of volunteers subjected to the most scrupulous and intimate of personal checks. Health officials demanded that everybody involved with the pie should consent to an excreta test. To a man, the Committee complied with all the stipulations, protecting the salubrity of the pie with military zeal. On the eve of the big day, a party of Whitehall officials arrived to carry out their final inspections. They were stopped in their tracks. Simmering in a barn, the pie was guarded by a lone sentry who challenged the visitors with the cry, 'As ta' ad thy shit tested? If thy 'asn't 'ad thy shit tested I've got a paper 'ere that sez tha can't come in.' The men from the ministry are reported to have left without a word!

Pie day was somewhat marred by traffic congestion and bad weather, and although large crowds were in attendance, ticket sales were not up to expectations and returns to local charities were a little disappointing, suggesting that the Yorkshire penchant for 'eating all and paying nowt' had been exercised in good measure.

Undeterred, the pie-men of Denby Dale are, as we

write, musing over the likely date of the ninth spectacular, casting urging eyes at the crown-less pate of our favourite prince. Should they fatten the herd now?

Yorkshire's Guillotine

Capital punishment takes many grisly forms. Perhaps the most chilling and well known is that introduced by Joseph Ignace Guillotine, a physician whose namesake saw such bloody service during the French Revolution. The shadow of the guillotine still haunts the Gallic shores, but what of Yorkshire's equally efficient device for decapitation? A by-word for Hell itself, the name of Halifax is eternally associated with its gibbet.

Surrounded by woods and wild moorland, 16th century Halifax was an increasingly prosperous town. Its fortunes were based on wool and the weaving, in isolated farmsteads, of fine quality cloths. These were delivered weekly to the town for finishing and dyeing and onward sale to merchants. Such was the demand for Halifax cloth and its high value, that delivery of the bolts became a precarious and dangerous occupation, criminals using the forest trails to ambush the weavers and steal their valuable wares. Alarmed at the increase in theft, the local judiciary introduced the severest of deterrents, decreeing that convicted villains apprehended with stolen cloth or goods to the value of 13½d or more should be executed.

The law prescribed that felons had to be caught with stolen goods in their possession and that arrests had to be made within the defined town boundaries covering the forest of Hardwick. It was the duty of the Bailiff to arrange a trial by jury, the evidence being 'solemnly and deliberately examined by the Frith Burghers'. Upon conviction, the condemned man was given six days to prepare for death. During this time he was exhibited in the town stocks as a public testimony to the folly of crime, his ill-gotten gains being displayed beside him. The humiliation ended with a final appointment with the gibbet, a macabre contrivance for removing heads, raised on a platform of stones and flags approached by steps.

Constructionally, the gibbet consisted of an axe fitted to a square section baulk of timber four and a half ft long. This was drawn by cord and pulley over a transverse beam supported between two upright posts. These were grooved on the inner faces to guide the axe to its mark. The axe was held by a pin attached to a line. If the misdemeanour had involved the theft of a beast, this line was in turn attached to the beast, which at the appointed time was whipped by the Bailiff. If no animals were involved, the rope was cut. Either way, death was quick, the seven pound twelve ounce axe making short work of its victims' necks.

After the execution, the coroner was required to summon the jury and carry out an inquest, recording the details of the execution in the official registers which list the names of 53 unfortunates beheaded between 20th March 1541 and 30th April 1650.

The origins of the gibbet are lost in the mists of time. There are several theories for its peculiar existence in

Halifax. Without doubt, ancient civilisations employed a similar technique for inflicting capital punishment, and it is suggested that the Norman barons also developed a machine for decapitation. Some say that the gibbet was inspired by the infamous Scottish Maiden in Edinburgh. Whatever the influences, the Halifax gibbet received a notoriety far beyond the confines of the forest of Hardwick.

As a means of deterrent it was unsurpassed, and the formalised legal rules of trial and testimony were highly regarded as an example of jurisprudence at its best. Due regard was given to confessions, and criminals could only be prosecuted if they were pursued by the aggrieved party . . . 'every man who had goods stolen should with or without the assistance of his friends or neighbours, pursue and endeavour to apprehend the thief, and if he were caught, the owner was not permitted to receive his goods again without prosecuting the felon; if he did so his goods were forfeited to the lord of the manor, and he was liable to be prosecuted for theft both for conniving and agreeing with the thief.' Another benefit was afforded the thief. If he managed to escape beyond the boundaries of the Hardwick, either before or after his trial, he was deemed safe and beyond reach of the gibbet. If, however, even after several years he returned to the parish, he still risked his head.

Without doubt, the gibbet was regarded with universal terror and awe. Surprisingly though, it had its plaudits outside Halifax, contemporaries speaking of 'A death so brave and manly that many persons of knightly order have petitioned the Kings of England that they might be honour'd with that Death, when condemn'd to suffer for their treasonable offences.' Law abiding Halifax residents had no such grave opinions. They seemed to have a fairly nonchalant attitude to executions, going about their business unconcerned and paying little attention to the terrible spectacles performed in their midst. One country woman on her way to market passed by the gibbet and found a severed head amongst the sweetmeats! And in later years, poems and plays were written about the gibbet, an 1837 theatrical performance celebrating the escape of a famous prisoner called Dennis.

The site of the Halifax gibbet was rediscovered in 1840. Today it is little more than a sinister grassy mound in the aptly named Gibbet Street. Some disciplinarians will mourn the passing of this grim reaper of heads. Most observers will, however, shudder and recite that well known extract from the vagrants' litany . . . 'From Hell, Hull and Halifax good Lord deliver us.'

The Festival of St Blaize

Honouring the patron saint of wool-combers, Bradford's festival of St Blaize was one of the most spectacular events in Europe. A colourful pageant symbolising the harmony between mill owners and their workers, the festival was held septennially between 1769 and 1825.

A former bishop of Sebaste in Armenia, Blaize is the reputed inventor of the craft of wool-combing. A cave dweller, he is said to have had a remarkable affinity with wild beasts, which were miraculously cured of sickness. Bishop Blaize was martyred in AD 316.

The great festival was held on the 3rd of February every seven years, the event calendar coinciding with the duration of apprenticeships for mill workers. The central theme of the convocation was a cavalcade, through streets thronged with spectators from the early hours. Strictly organised, each profession being allotted its individual place, the procession was a riot of flags and finery.

'The apprentices and masters' sons . . . formed the most showy part of the procession; their caps being richly ornamented with ostrich feathers, flowers, and knots of various coloured yarn; and their stuff garments formed of the gayest colours. Some of these dresses were very costly, from the profusion of their decorations.

The shepherd, shepherdess, and swains were attired in bright green. The woolsorters, from their number, and the height of their plumes of feathers, which were mostly of different colours, formed in the shape of a fleur-de-lis, had a dashing appearance. The comb-makers carried before them the instruments here so much celebrated, raised on standards, together with golden fleeces, rams' heads with gilded horns and other emblems. The wool-combers were neatly dressed, and looked mighty wise in their odd-fashioned and full flowing wigs of combed wool.'

The processional order was as follows:

'Herald, bearing a flag.
Twenty-four Woolstaplers on horseback, each horse caparisoned with a fleece.
Thirty-eight Worsted-spinners and Manufacturers on horseback, in white stuff waistcoats, with each a sliver of wool over his shoulder and a white stuff sash; the horses' necks covered with nets made of thick yarn.
Six Merchants on horseback, with coloured sashes.
Three Guards. Masters' Colours. Three Guards.
Fifty-six Apprentices and Masters' Sons on horseback, with ornamented caps, scarlet coloured coats, white stuff waistcoats, and blue pantaloons.
Bradford and Keighley bands.

Macebearer, on foot.
Six Guards. KING. QUEEN. Six Guards.
Guards. JASON. PRINCESS MEDEA. Guards.
Bishop's Chaplain.
BISHOP BLAIZE.
Shepherd and Shepherdess.
Shepherd-Swains,
One hundred and sixty Woolsorters on horseback,
with ornamented caps and various coloured slivers.
Thirty Comb-makers.
Charcoal Burners.
Combers' Colours.
Band.
Forty Dyers, with red cockades, blue aprons, and
crossed slivers of red and blue.'

The whole tumultuous entourage took several hours to complete its course. There then followed a banquet, paid for by the mill owners. In later years, the drunken propensities of the large crowds earned the festival a bad name.

In 1825, the year of the last festival proper, over 800 manufacturers participated in an event soured by increasing tensions and disharmony. The craft of spinning had already been mechanised, and the workers feared further mechanisation and job losses. Contrary to the sentiments of a hymn specially written for the festival — 'Our rising commerce now her arms extends; The rich she blesses and the poor befriends' — the after dinner speeches reflected the growing concerns, and within a few weeks the local economy was devastated by a lengthy strike lasting 23 weeks.

Forty eight years later, memories of Bradford's

colourful history were recalled, and the council decided to organise another festival to mark the opening of the new Town Hall, inviting representatives from all local trades.

With meticulous planning, 17 bands, 93 trade waggons with emblematic devices, 90 carriages, 20 banners, 153 mounted riders and 6,453 persons on foot set out from Lister Park at ten o'clock on 9th September 1873. Immediately, a problem arose. To the great annoyance of their drivers, the vehicles representing the coal and glass and china dealers had not been allocated places in the procession. Ignominiously tagged onto the rear of the cavalcade, bearing a highly inappropriate banner emblazoned 'Onward!', these drivers fumed, the less sensitive observers enjoying a string of expletives. And then it rained and a further complication contrived to ruin the day. The residents of the Manchester Road and Little Horton areas were annoyed because the route of the procession did not pass their homes. As a symbol of their disgust, they erected a banner across Manchester Road. The message read 'Pity Horton; it has a population of 40,000 and cannot be favoured with a sight of the procession.' The resentment of the crowds was musically expressed by a brass band which approached the Town Hall playing the Dead March and other funeral airs!

Despite the setbacks and the interminable after dinner speeches, the Town Hall was opened with great pomp and ceremony. As darkness fell it was bathed in gaslight and celebrations lasted well into the night. For several days afterwards, the whole town was decked with flags and bunting. A gala was held in

Manningham Park and a firework display entertained 20,000 people in Peel Park.

Since 1873, the civic pride of Bradford has been somewhat muted . . . but in these heritage conscious times might St Blaize's standard be raised again?

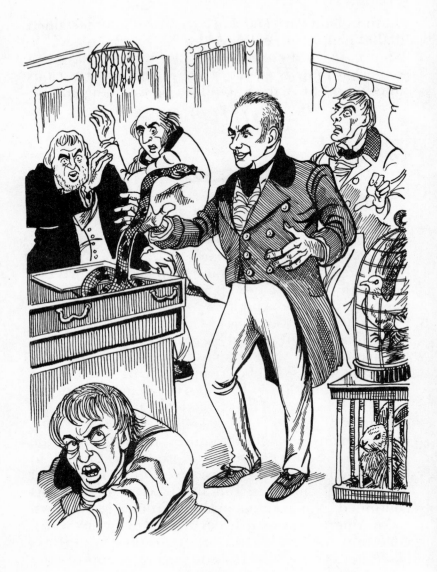

The Snake-Charming Squire

Born in 1782 at Walton Hall near Wakefield, Charles Waterton was one of the most colourful eccentrics of his age. Naturalist, explorer, perfecter of the taxidermal art, an experimenter with the native poison curare, and a lifelong prankster, he is credited with founding the world's first nature reserve. Waterton had an incredible passion for life and a fascination with wild animals. An escapade in 1820 involving an Essequibo river cayman, the hapless creature being ridden Epsom style, demonstrates the Squire's relish for danger, and his appetite for the outlandish.

After many notable adventures, particularly in the jungles of South America, Waterton returned to Yorkshire to spend a comparatively quiet retirement with scalpel and pen. But the hair-raising exploits continued, as an incident in Leeds around 1834 shows.

An American animal dealer arrived in the city with a collection of 28 deadly rattlesnakes. Waterton's associate, a Dr Richard Hobson, seeing an opportunity to assess the antidotal properties of curare and to compare its effects with those of snake venom, arranged an evening of experimentation, inviting Waterton and over 40 local doctors to attend. Numerous guinea pigs, rabbits and pigeons were readied for their ordeal, and the snakes, in a specially constructed case separated into compartments, were brought in.

Agog, the company waited for the action to begin, but a problem arose. How would the obviously reluctant victims be held within fang range without the safety of the handler being jeopardised? Perplexed, the entire assembly, including the American dealer, refused to volunteer their hands, until, in frustration, the Squire stepped forward and offered his services.

There was a deathly hush as Hobson gingerly raised the lid of one of the compartments. Very slowly Waterton inserted his unprotected fist into the case, quickly grasping a snake behind the neck as its agitated fellows, preparing to strike, hissed and rattled loudly. The lid was closed, the rattlesnake was induced to bite its prey and was soon returned to the box. There was a communal sigh of relief.

With little hesitation by Waterton, but with a mounting anxiety on the part of the audience, the performance was repeated a number of times using different victims. Then, abruptly, one of the snakes make a dart for freedom, half escaping the box just as Waterton was retrieving his hand. In dire panic, all the learned doctors apart from Hobson fled the room, some rushing blindly into the street without their hats.

Curbing his natural inclination to slam the box shut and risk multiple bites to Waterton's trapped hand,

Hobson gently lowered the lid to prevent the renegade snake from escaping completely. This gave Waterton the time to withdraw his hand and in one movement to coolly return the enraged reptile to its lair.

Apart from demonstrating the Squire's unflappable courage and icy nerve, the experiment revealed little, other than to show that curare poison acted more quickly than venom. However, to the derision of many, the trials continued over a number of years.

Despite being perceived as an amateurish buffoon by some more qualified scientists and medical researchers of his day, Waterton persevered. Suffice to say that in June 1982 on the bicentenary of his birth, the Yorkshire Society of Anaesthetists felt it appropriate to hold their symposium at Walton Hall.

The Bingley War

Spawned by political repression, the passing of the Poor Law Act, and by an economic slump, the national Chartist movement was formed in 1836. Demanding six political reforms, principally universal suffrage, secret ballots and annual parliaments, the Chartists sparked a social revolution, contested in Bingley by blunderbuss-sloping Chelsea pensioners, who were in the vanguard of the fray.

In Yorkshire, the Chartist banner was flown by such leaders as Fergus O'Connor who roused his followers with the greeting 'Ye famished beings in rags!' Exhorted to action, those of the 'fustian jackets, blistered hands and unshorn chins' perpetrated a series of reckless attacks on the mills, brandishing shillelaghs, pitchforks, sticks and iron bars and descending in great numbers to disable the steam boilers. In Bingley, as elsewhere, the wreckers ran amok, but on the 26th May 1848, two of the ringleaders were captured in the town. The arrests stirred the already militant Chartists to action.

In shackles, the prisoners were brought before the Petty Sessions, curiously held above the Brown Cow tavern. The indictments were read, but the proceedings were violently interrupted. A mob broke down the door, threatening to murder the presiding magistrate, Squire Ferrand, who with great courage said 'If you murder me, another will take my place, who will discharge his duties as resolutely as I have done.' Renewing their threats, the intruders carried their comrades off in triumph to a smithy, where the shackles were hammered off. Fully intending to keep their murderous vow, the crowd lay in wait, expecting to ambush the magistrate on his way home. Fortunately, the gentleman was forewarned. He took a detour and returned to his house unmolested. In furious pique, the Chartists mutilated one of the Squire's favourite ash trees, and they fell on a wayside water trough, cutting it up to make bullets. The prospects looked grim.

Vast rallies haranguing the 'bloated aristocracy' continued to be held in the district, and on 10th April 1848, when Fergus O'Conner presented his two million signature petition to Parliament, such was the fear of wholesale uprising in Bingley, that the government saw fit to despatch over 100 old contemptibles, gouty pensioners of the Chelsea brigade (one with a wooden leg!) armed with rusty and equally venerable matchlock rifles. They were billeted in the town, private households and inns accommodating two soldiers each.

The first military clash with the Chartists followed a riot. Led by Squire Ferrand, the soldiers arrested 16 of the principal agitators, and they were committed to York Castle, and taken to the railway station to await transportation. In view of the success of past rescue attempts, the platform was well guarded and all the prisoners were safely locked in the specially chartered train. Before it steamed away one of the men shouted to the crowd, 'Go tell that blind lad of mine that his father's gone to die a martyr for his country.'

Some days after the riot, large numbers of Chartists converged on Toftshaw Moor. A body of dragoons galloped to the scene and cutlasses were drawn in an attempt to restore order. Thankfully, there was very little violence, the only casualty being the hat of a simple fellow from Micklethwaite. Cut in half by deft swordsmanship, the hat was the cause of much mirth.

A second amusing incident helped dispel the gloom. Hot foot from Barden Moor, a man descended one Sunday morning with desperate news, reporting that a multitude of Chartists were mobilising for an attack on Bingley. Services in the town were instantly stopped, the alarm bells were rung and a great posse of men, some trembling with fear, were led off by the redoubtable Squire. What a reception! The reported massing of troops was, in reality, a gathering of Primitive Methodists at prayer!

Further confrontation in what became known as the Bingley War was limited. There had been much fierce argument, invective, rancour and a handful of arrests, but happily little bloodshed. Squire Ferrand had dealt with often volatile and dangerous situations with firmness and sympathy, and his efforts in maintaining comparative peace were acknowledged by a grateful government.

Bradford's
Spectral Saviour

With typical Yorkshire phlegm, the independent citizens of Bradford have long been noted for their pluck and determination. Unaided, they have over the centuries resisted fire, flood, pestilence and armed attack. In 1643, however, against seemingly overwhelming odds the annihilation of the entire population looked certain . . . but then a spectral lady appeared.

During the English Civil War, to its cost, Bradford allied with Cromwell and the Parliamentarians. After the battle of Adwalton Moor in 1643, the victorious Royalist commander, the Earl of Newcastle, besieged the town, commandeering the nearby Bolling Hall as his headquarters. Encircling the Roundhead positions with his cannon, the earl unleashed a barrage of fire, confident of an early capitulation. Resolutely, the defenders took up position in their parish church, converting it into a fortress and hanging woolsacks from the tower to deflect the shot.

For three days, the battle raged, the Earl of Newcastle becoming so outraged at the defiance against superior forces that he resolved to slaughter the entire garrison. Having expended the last of 26 barrels of gunpowder,

the gallant fighters of this Battle of the Steeple prepared themselves for the final assault as the sun set. A contemporary lament records their tragic plight: 'Oh! What a night and morning was that in which Bradford was taken! What weeping and wringing of hands! None expecting to live any longer than till the enemy came into town; the Earl of Newcastle having charged his men to kill all, man, woman, and child. . . .'

Meanwhile, confident of the morn, the Earl of Newcastle prepared for bed in Bolling Hall. He retired to a finely plastered room, gazing at a frieze dancing with images of human heads and grotesque animals. But he would have no rest this night. Sleep proved impossible, for a ghostly lady dressed in white repeatedly pulled off his bed clothes and implored the frightened earl to 'Pity poor Bradford! Pity poor Bradford!'

> Mournful she seemed though young and fair
> She clasped her hands, as if in prayer
> And, sighing, said 'in pity spare
> Our poor devoted town.'

The pleading spectre of the night shook the earl's resolve, and in the morning, to the surprise of his troops and to the incredulous delight of the Roundheads, he despatched a trumpeter to negotiate a truce. Terms were agreed and the people of Bradford were saved.

The identity of the benevolent spirit has never been established. Some 70 years ago a psychic research specialist spent a night in the old hall in an attempt to rouse the lady, but his vigil went unrewarded. She sleeps still. Can only an imperilled Bradford wake her?

The Turnpike Riots

Stubborn and independent, the traditional Tyke is fiercely resistant of change. Add a pecuniary element to the equation and the consequences can be dire indeed.

In the 18th century, the roads of our county were in a deplorable state. Rutted and barely wide enough to permit the passage of a single carriage, the insubstantial highways were dangerous and uncertain arteries of communication, highly prone to obliteration in bad weather. Recognising the problems, Parliament encouraged the enactment of local by-laws, investing the power of road construction, management and repair in trustees or commissioners, whose immediate priority was to raise funds. Enter the toll-road.

The hitherto inalienable right of free passage was suddenly denied, and the population of West Yorkshire, particularly the working classes of Bradford and Leeds, were incensed. From time immemorial they had passed unhindered on albeit treacherous roads, but their journeys had been free and the thought of paying for the privilege of travelling caused widespread unrest.

The newly designated turnpike roads were controlled by manned toll-houses, collection points where access was restricted by broad white gates. Adding fuel to the discontent was the realisation that the toll-houses were an enterprise of wealthy businessmen or the aristocracy, the widely held perception being that the imposition of toll-fees was a further exploitation of the poorest members of society. The final insult to the by now seething populace was the possibility under turnpike legislation of toll collectors seizing horses for their own benefit if the prescribed number of steeds allowed for certain classes of team were exceeded. There was an irresistible call to riot.

By early June 1753, the masses were on the move. Targeting their wrath against the despised toll-houses, a large mob marched from Leeds to Halton Dial on the York Road and inflicted great damage. Emboldened, a 300 strong contingent of men armed with swords and clubs moved on, intent on demolishing the bar at Harewood Bridge. The resultant pitched battle was the prelude to one of the bloodiest days of civil unrest in the history of Leeds.

Approaching from Weardley, the rioters were met by an 80 strong force of tenants and workmen with the Earl of Harewood at their head. Protestations and abuse soon gave way to armed conflict at Mill Green, a field not far from the bar, and in the ensuing fight there were heinous injuries on both sides. Despite their inferiority in numbers, the earl's men managed to win the day, taking 30 prisoners, ten of whom were eventually incarcerated in York Castle. Exasperated at the defeat, the mob retreated. Further violence was threatened and a squadron of dragoons was sent from York for the final showdown.

One week later, a carter, who had refused to pay a toll, was arrested by soldiers at the Beeston turnpike gates in Leeds. The man was rescued by an angry crowd who converged later in the day on the King's Arms Inn in Briggate, Leeds, where three other prisoners were arraigned for refusing to pay tolls. About seven o'clock in the evening a boisterous rabble assembled outside the inn and began attacking the guarding soldiers with stones and paving slabs. Windows and shutters were broken and in the melee, made worse by the curiosity of Saturday night crowds, a dragoon was knocked to the ground. In desperation, the mayor was summoned. The Riot Act was read, a curfew was imposed and all the local shops were ordered to shut. But the aggression grew worse. Reluctantly, the soldiers were ordered to load their weapons.

Using powder only, the first tactic was to frighten the crowd into dispersal. The volley had no effect, other than to rouse the rioters into renewed frenzy. At last, the levelled muskets were loaded with live ammunition and after a final warning, a fusillade rent the night air. Contemporary accounts of the assault differ in the numbers of rioters said to have been either killed or injured, but all the reports speak of brutal carnage with many men lying dead or dying. The cause of the turnpike rioters was dealt a fatal blow and they never again launched a major assault on the offending gates, although animosity against the mayor and other officials lasted for years.

After this milestone event, the improvement of the

local highway system made greater progress. Traffic increased and there was a gradual growth of regular coaching services. The inclinations of classically parsimonious Yorkshiremen, however, led to the development of the off-road horse!

'Old Three Laps'

The Worlds Farm in the lonely hamlet of Laycock near Keighley was once the home of a jilted bridegroom, who in the first half of the 19th century endured a marathon sentence of pining that would have put Dickens' Miss Faversham to shame.

'Old Three Laps' inherited his unusual nick-name from his eccentric father, a tight-fisted yeoman farmer who, in need of a coat, one day visited a Keighley tailor. On measuring the farmer, the tailor discovered that he had insufficient cloth to complete the coat. Perplexed, he asked for instructions. 'Tho' mun make it three laps' (in colloquial parlance 'any way'), replied the farmer, who was immediately tagged with the new name.

For a while, the farmer's son was occupied as a weaver, but he was a dissolute lad who preferred roaming the moors and drinking at the Devonshire Inn in Keighley to following an honest trade. The ale was not the only distraction, however, and he fell desperately in love with a barmaid, the comely daughter of a neighbouring farmer. After a whirlwind courtship, he proposed marriage and the date for the wedding was fixed. In great excitement, the bridegroom arrived at Keighley church for the ceremony, and he waited, and he waited, but the bride did not appear. Shortly before the nuptials a dispute had arisen between the respective fathers about the dowry, and unbeknown to the expectant groom the wedding had been cancelled. Devastated, the groom went home to bed where he stayed for 49 years!

'Old Three Laps' was 39 years old when he retired. Shutting himself in a tiny stone flagged room, he vowed he would speak to no-one, even ignoring his constant attendants provided from the proceeds of his father's will.

In his dreary damp cell, furnished with a four-poster bed without hangings, a dark oak table and a cobwebbed clock bereft of its weight and pendulum, the recluse eked out an existence. Surprisingly for a man so confined, he ate well, although his manner of dining was extremely odd. Upon receiving his food he would assume a kneeling posture, after eating, cavorting with his plate in the fashion of a juggler.

Over the years, denied light, exercise and any semblance of social contact, the old man became a hideous skulking beast, retreating to the oblivion of his bedclothes whenever a stranger entered his den. A gentleman who visited the farm shortly before 'Old Three Laps' death has left us the following grisly account:—

'To gain admission we had some difficulty; but with the assistance of the farmer and a tin of tobacco to the nurse, who was an inveterate smoker, we were shown into his bedroom. As soon as he heard strangers, he pulled back the bed clothes over his head, which the nurse with considerable force removed, and uncovered his body, which was devoid of every vestige of body linen. A more startling and sickening sight I never saw. "Three Laps" covered his face with his hands, his fingers being like birds' claws, while, with his legs drawn under his body, he had the appearance of a huge beast. He had white hair, and a very handsome head, well set on a strong chest. His body and all about him was scrupulously clean, and his condition healthy, as his nurse proudly pointed out, digging her fist furiously into his ribs. He gave no signs of joy or pain, but lay like a mass of inanimate matter.'

About a week before his death, 'Old Three Laps' began to fail. Shortly before the fatal hour on 3rd March 1856, he was heard to exclaim — 'Poor Bill! poor Bill! poor Bill Sharp!' Ejaculating the most complete sentence he had uttered in 49 years, the old man died.

Attended by large inquisitive crowds who had come from far and wide to witness the scene, the body was interred in Keighley churchyard, a place 'Old Three Laps' had once visited with such hopes.

The extraordinary coffin, specially built to accommodate a 17 stone corpse, whose twisted limbs could not be straightened, caused considerable excitement. Made from oak, and measuring two feet four inches in depth, the coffin required the strength of eight men and thick ropes to lower it into the grave.

'Old Three Laps' paid a heavy price for love. Perhaps he plighted his troth in heaven?

The Marque of Jowett

Squeezed to extinction by competition and the imperatives of mass production, West Yorkshire's own motor manufacturing industry has long since passed into the annals of history, and only the name of Jowett, kept bright by a handful of enthusiasts, lives on.

The Kestrel, the Flat Four, and the incomparable Javelin, all had their unlikely origins in Bradford's Manningham Lane, where a small motor cycle business had been founded by brothers Benjamin and William Jowett at the turn of the century.

The dawning of the motor age had fired the ambition of the partners, and acquiring rudimentary machine tools, they produced a six-horsepower, two-cylinder, two-seater water-cooled vehicle as a prototype. Registered in 1906 and probably the first British light car, this Jowett had eye-catching lines, box seats, a large hood and acetylene lamps. An instant success, it generated a rash of orders. To meet demand, the brothers moved to new premises in Grosvenor Road, Bradford in 1910, and the Jowett Motor Manufacturing Company was born.

Diverted into the manufacture of armaments

during the First World War, production of the moderately priced (£152 5s 0d) cars slowed, but in 1919 the business was transferred to a purpose built and specially equipped factory in Idle, and volume production began.

Jowett cars developed an enviable reputation for astounding power from the smallest of engines, for reliability, fuel economy and longevity, and it was even claimed that the vehicles were passed on as family heirlooms, such was the quality of construction. Constantly being improved (two colours were available — blue, and green-grey, both applied by hand), the aluminium-bodied vehicles came off the production line at the rate of ten per week. Before delivery, they were subjected to a five mile road test. Proud owners were presented with a tin of matching paint for subsequent touching up!

In 1923, production expanded to 15 cars per week, and vehicles were protected with nickel plating as standard. Drivers with an aversion to bad backs and the infamous starting handles, could, for an extra £15 on top of the £220 purchase price, opt for electric starting.

In response to public demand, a four-seater car, the 'Long Four' was introduced and production rocketed to over 60 units per week by the end of 1925. Incredibly roomy, although it had only two doors, both on the near side, the new vehicle and its successors were widely applauded by the motoring press. Spurred on to greater heights, the Jowett brothers experimented with a sports car which in 1928 captured the International and British Class G Twelve Hour Record at Brooklands at an average speed of 54.86 mph.

111

Each year saw advancements in specification and design, but in 1931 a disastrous fire destroyed much of the factory, the flames engulfing a number of highly secret show cars which had been prepared for delivery the following year. Working under open skies, with great determination, the cars were stripped down to the last nut, refurbished and rebuilt, and within six months production levels were restored.

The Kestrel, a light, four-seater car with a swept tail, took wing in 1931, and this was followed in 1936 by the introduction of the revolutionary 'Flat Four', a horizontally opposed four-cylinder vehicle boasting ten horsepower.

Towards the end of the 1930s, however, competitive pressures affected sales, especially in the export market, and it became increasingly apparent that without radical restructuring the business would not survive the post war years. Reluctantly, the Jowett brothers retired, passing control of the company to the financier Sir Charles Clore.

Acknowledging the need to retain a share in the ever increasing market, during the war years the new directors commissioned a former pupil of the world famous designer Issigonis to prepare a brief for an advanced car. Working secretly in a back room at the Idle plant, Gerald Palmer was set the task of designing a completely new car with the advanced appeal of a Citroen. The only other stipulation was the price tag — under £500.

The subject of endless changes, speculation and advance publicity, the new vehicle was finally unveiled to an astonished British market in 1947. The mould breaking Jowett Javelin was on the road!

Sensationally modern in appearance and construction, the 1½ litre, four-seater Javelin could achieve a maximum speed of nearly 80 mph and public demand was insatiable. As a post war austerity measure, the car was reserved for doctors, farmers, diplomats or for genuine export. Several people were arrested for attempting illegal purchase, and it was only when supplies of steel and other essential materials eased that production began in earnest. A motoring journalist on a rare journey north has left us the following impressions of the excitement caused by this pride of Idle.

'The good folk up Idle way . . . scarcely anticipated that their brainchild would become one of the high spots of the post war motoring world. Cheque books are outed and fountain pens flourished as if people were afraid they wouldn't get in first. Acceleration will satisfy those who like to get off the mark at "robows" as traffic lights are called by the man-in-the-street in Yorkshire, and it is gratifying to sit in a British light car that can give the big Yank jobs a surprise when the colours change.'

Uprated, and joined by its stable mate the Jupiter, the Javelin went on to become one of the thoroughbred cars of the age. But success was short lived. Regrettably, Jowett Cars Ltd succumbed to overwhelming competition and the factory was closed forever in 1954.

In the 1990s, Jowett's indelible marques survive, cherished by a band of owners' club members who recall the thrill of the open road. Symbols of a more carefree age of motoring, the Javelins purr on.

113

The Battle of
Wakefield Green

The great feudal contest for the supremacy of
England known as the Wars of the Roses, spilt as
much Yorkshire blood as any conflict in history. A
dynastic fight between the rival houses of York and
Lancaster, made worse by local feuds between the
nobility, the wars lasted 30 years between 1455 and
1485, when the decisive meeting at Bosworth Field
ended in triumph for Henry Tudor.

A bloody interlude in the carnage took place on
Tuesday, 30th December 1460 at Wakefield Green.
The Duke of York, with 5,000 followers of the white
rose, had spent a bleak Christmas in Sandal Castle
awaiting reinforcements from the south. Attempting
to augment his forces, the duke had commissioned a
kinsman to recruit an additional 8,000 men, but with
great treachery the forces were persuaded to swell the
ranks of Queen Margaret's opposing Lancastrian
army stationed at Pontefract Castle some nine miles to
the east. With a total contingent of 20,000 men, the red
rose was set to sweep the field.

Determined to seize the initiative, the Lancastrians
ordered their troops forward. The Yorkists,
meanwhile, needing to replenish their diminishing

stocks of food, sent out a foraging party to buy provisions from local farmers. Victualled, the small band sped for the sanctuary of the castle, but they were intercepted and attacked by a division under the command of Lord Clifford.

Called to the ramparts, the Duke of York grieved at the plight of his men. Thinking that he spied the entire Lancastrian army, contrary to the advice of his most experienced officer Sir David Hall, he resolved to attempt a rescue. 'A Davy, a Davy!' he admonished. 'Hast thou loved me so long and now wouldst thou have me dishonoured . . . I thank God, and to my honour. For surely my mind is rather to die with honour than live with shame. Of honour cometh fame, and of dishonour ariseth infamy. Therefore advance my banner, in the name of God and Saint George, for surely I will fight with them, though I should fight alone!'

In a blinding snowstorm, the drawbridge was lowered and the Yorkists marched out, a falcon-emblazoned banner at their head. Flights of Lancastrian arrows pierced the blizzard and the battle was joined, fierce hand to hand fighting driving the attackers towards the river Calder. For a while, the contest was evenly matched, then, summoned by their vigilant scouts, the main Lancastrian army lying in ambush at Milnthorpe to the south, deployed in a classical pincer movement, surrounding the Yorkists and cutting them to pieces. Hacking and stabbing in bloody frenzy the Lancastrians gave no quarter but the gallant duke rallied his men. 'Charge! and give no foot of ground, a crown, or else a glorious tomb! a sceptre, or an earthly sepulchre.'

In the brutal melee, the duke and 2,000 of his men

were slain. The victor, Lord Clifford (he well deserved the title 'Bloody Clifford'), surveyed the battlefield, and, after the barbarous custom of those times, he cut off the duke's head with his sword. The grisly trophy was subjected to the most appalling mockery and insult, the triumphant soldiers crowning the head with sedges and bullrushes and crying in derision 'Hail, King without rule! Hail, King without heritage! Hail, Duke and Prince without people!'

The atrocities were not yet done. The Duke of York's seven year old second son, prominent in his regal garb, was escaping the battlefield when he was intercepted by Lord Clifford. Speechless, the boy dropped to his knees in fear. 'Save him,' begged the royal chaplain, 'for he is a prince's son, and may peradventure do you good hereafter.' Realising the identity of his prisoner, Lord Clifford was consumed with hatred and stabbed the boy to the heart with his dagger, uttering the words 'By God's blood thy father slew my father, and so will I thee and all thy kin, therefore die!'

The headless corpse of the Duke of York was taken to be buried in the church of the Cluniac Priory of St John in Pontefract. The bodies of his men were tossed into deep trenches dug in a field near the castle and as the day ended, 'the kindly snow fell like a mantle on the dead and covered the rueful faces staring so fiercely to Heaven.'

In the final degrading spectacle, the duke's head was spiked on Micklegate Bar in York. Bearing a paper crown, the head was jeered at, its face turned towards the city with the taunt 'So York may overlook the town of York.'

116

Marched to the Tower of London the Yorkist survivors of the battle were incarcerated in a dungeon renamed the Wakefield Tower, as the Wars of the Roses raged on.

Revenge, so they say, is sweet, and three months after the Battle of Wakefield Green the adversaries met again. In the bloodiest battle ever fought on English soil, at Towton near Tadcaster, the Lancastrians were slaughtered in great numbers, 'Bloody Clifford' dying the night before the action from wounds inflicted by an arrow.

On 22nd July 1466, King Edward IV honoured his father's body with a spendid funeral. The remains of the Duke of York were exhumed and carried in a chariot to Fotheringay, where a requiem mass was said. In memory of his father, the king also erected crosses in Sandal and in Kirkgate, Wakefield, and many years later, the citizens of Wakefield raised their own permanent memorial on part of the Manygates School site:

'Richard Plantagenet, Duke of York, fighting for the cause of the White Rose, fell on this spot in the Battle of Wakefield, December 30th 1460.
This stone is erected in 1897 by some who wish to preserve the traditional site.'

The precise spot where the duke fell was long marked by three forlorn willow trees. Although the trees were lost to a storm in 1866 they are still remembered in an old local saying — 'Mind the Duke of York without his head doesn't git hod o' thee as tha gans by the willow trees.'

The Vision of Titus Salt

❧

The statue of Sir Titus Salt stares out across the river at Saltaire, the model village creation of an industrial philanthropist who inspired the world.

Titus was born into an iron-founding and textile manufacturing family on 20th September 1803. The first of seven children, he was educated at a dame school in Morley near Leeds, eventually being transferred to academies in Batley and Wakefield.

Leaving school in 1820, Titus was first apprenticed to a wool-comber in Wakefield. He moved to Bradford in 1822 to gain further experience in worsted spinning and completed the first phase of a promising career by accompanying his father on business expeditions to London and Liverpool, and to farms in Norfolk and Lincolnshire.

Demonstrating a concern for his fellow man which was to colour all his subsequent ventures, Titus, fired by his strict chapel upbringing, helped found the Mechanics Institute. He also intervened in a Luddite revolt, risking personal injury in an attempt to explain the benefits of mechanisation.

In 1836, fate and not a little business intuition, sparked the young Salt. Three hundred bales of inferior alpaca wool had been languishing in a Liverpool warehouse unwanted until, at a bargain price, Titus bought the entire consignment, to the consternation and utter amazement of his father and the profession at large. Adapting the manufacturing process, Titus succeeded in producing top quality yarn, blending his alpaca with cotton and dazzling the market with whole new ranges of beautiful cloths.

Committed to the local community, in 1844 Titus became the mayor of Bradford. He contemplated retiring from business some two years later, but a change of heart led him into the architectural adventure of the age. The drive for greater efficiency persuaded him of the merits of concentrating all his production in one modern mill, preferably located away from the urban problems of Bradford. A green field site was chosen near Shipley and plans for the model village of Saltaire were drawn up.

An Italianate design was approved for the new six storey mill. This was opened in 1853 and was celebrated with an enormous banquet. Workers' housing, incorporating many features specifically requested by the employees themselves, was completed by 1872.

Compared to the jerry built slums in Bradford, the new cottage homes were veritable palaces and outside amenities were not overlooked. The streets were built to generous widths and were properly paved with stone. Drainage conformed to the latest sanitary principles. An infirmary was erected, communal baths and a wash-house were provided (the facilities included six steam-driven washing machines and a spin drier!) and latterly, school buildings, a Wesleyan chapel and a splendid Congregational church were begun. The prestigious development was crowned by the construction of 40 shops (but no public house!), a large reading room with a library boasting 8,500 books, and a magnificent 14 acre riverside park with facilities for swimming, games and boating. Such was the deserved reputation of Saltaire that people from all over the globe came to inspect Salt's vast creation.

In 1859, Titus was elected as Liberal Member for Bradford, but his constituency duties were short lived. Ill health caused him to relinquish his seat, and leaving the running of his business to his three sons, he retired gracefully to cultivate fruit and flowers in his hothouses.

To celebrate the twentieth anniversary of the opening of the factory a grand event was organised in 1873. The residents of Saltaire were entertained by three brass bands, and a great tent was erected to accommodate 4,200 guests. The principal guest at the festivities, who enjoyed his 70th birthday that very day, was toasted in 140 pounds of tea and 60 gallons of milk!

A wealthy but a generous and kindhearted man, Titus Salt reluctantly accepted public recognition for his sterling achievements in 1869. Sir Titus continued his charitable works to the end, endowing his riches on orphanages, hospitals, and schools. He died in 1876, people in their thousands flocking to pay tribute to a man who had finally slain the ogre of the dark satanic mill.

The Coiners of Cragg Vale

Within curlew cry of the Lancashire border, only minutes from the thunderous M62, lies Cragg Vale; brooding, precipitous and still. From Mythomroyd the vale companions the Cragg Brook, labouring past scattered farmsteads, the former roosts of some of the vilest criminals in Yorkshire history. The story of these counterfeiters, or 'Cragg Coiners' as they are known today, has been romanticised in recent years, but the facts tell a different tale.

At the beginning of the 18th century, such was the laborious preoccupation with foreign wars, that the national coinage had long been neglected. New issues by the Mint were badly worn and reduced in size, and portable balances for calculating the reduced value of coins became commercial necessities, as did the use of substitute foreign coins from Spain and Portugal. The climate for the unscrupulous paring or clipping of coins, and the manufacture of counterfeit money from the proceeds, was rife, and gangs throughout the country worked a profitable trade, duping many who failed to recognise the bogus from the real.

During the 1760s, Halifax and district was ideal territory for coiners, being a regional centre for

commerce with remote places for coin manufacture within easy reach. The farmhouses of Cragg Vale were particularly suitable, offering isolation, anonymity, and opportunities for long distance surveillance to warn of intruders.

The leader of the 'Cragg Coiners' was experienced metal worker David Hartley, or 'King David' as he was known to his 70 strong band. Hartley, who lived in Bell House, a small farmhouse overlooking the picturesque Bell Hole, was the inspiration for the lucrative production of fake Portuguese moidores, chosen in preference to English coins for several important reasons. Firstly, although moidores were acceptable currency, their rarity made comparison with bogus coins difficult. Secondly, since no moidores had been issued since 1722, contemporary stocks were 40 years old, and they showed signs of wear, which allowed the poor replicas to pass unnoticed. The final reason for choosing the moidore, perhaps the most compelling, was in the simple geometry of its design, allowing relatively easy die making.

The process of counterfeiting began with the purchase of full sized golden guineas for 22 shillings, the shady innkeepers of the district being a good source of supply. Using shears, gold shavings were removed from the edges of these coins. They were then filed round, and roughly re-milled before being re-introduced into circulation. The gold shavings were collected, smelted and finally struck with rudimentary hand tools to produce moidores by the hundred, reaping a profit of about a pound for every seven guineas clipped.

Gradually the Halifax coinage was debased to such

123

an extent that outsiders became reluctant to trade, and several local manufacturers petitioned the government to act. Lack of government funds brought a negative response, but a further approach by exciseman William Dighton resulted in a promise of official help.

Encouraged by a Halifax solicitor, Dighton harried the gang, engaging the services of an informer named James Broadbent, whose treachery led to the arrest of Hartley and a fellow coiner named James Jagger. The men were sent to York castle under heavy guard to await trial.

Broadbent meanwhile, under duress from Hartley's family, attempted to retract his evidence, but the damage had been done and the prisoners remained in York, whilst their associates sought to eliminate Dighton. This they did in Halifax on the night of 10th November 1769, when assassins Robert Thomas and Matthew Normanton despatched the exciseman with a single blunderbuss shot to the head. Under cover of darkness the killers stole personal effects and cruelly kicked the corpse, leaving a trail of foot-prints on the wet ground.

Stung into action at the murder of one of their officials, the government offered a reward of £100 for the arrest of the murderers. A further £100 was added by the gentlemen and merchants of Halifax, and only 16 days after the outrage, a government appointee, the Marquis of Rockingham, organised a mass meeting of concerned nobility and gentry from Halifax, Bradford, Leeds and Wakefield. The meeting persuaded many gentlemen to become JPs, and the relentless pursuit of the coiners continued, resulting in the arrest of some 30 suspects by Christmas.

Tempted by the £200 reward, Broadbent again surfaced, to reveal the names of Dighton's murderers, his evidence being corroborated by 'King David', who was anxious to save his own skin. The gang leader's testimony was, however, to no effect, and he was summarily hanged at York on 28th April 1770.

The trial of the murderers began in August, but Broadbent's vacillating evidence was flawed, arousing doubts which led to acquittal.

Disdainful of the law, the gang rather stupidly continued their evil ways, reaching new heights of barbarity with the murder of a labourer in Heptonstall. Whilst in the company of several coiners, the man had foolishly claimed he knew the identities of Dighton's murderers. The contemporary account of the labourer's demise is horrific. '. . . they immediately threw him against the fire and thrust his head into or under it . . . one of them heated the tongs red hot, clasping them fast around the poor creature's neck, and kept them there . . . but their inhumanity not being yet satiated, they actually filled his breeches with burning coals by which the poor fellow died in the greatest of agonies.'

With such heinous behaviour inciting public storm, the coiners' days were numbered. Arrests became commonplace, and in 1774 in connection with the robbery and murder of Dighton, four men were arrested, including the previously arraigned Thomas and Normanton. Having already been acquitted of murder under English law, Thomas and Normanton could not be prosecuted for the same offence. They were, however, both found guilty of highway robbery, an offence for which they paid the ultimate price.

Within a few years, the reign of the coiners had been ended, 'King David's' tombstone in the churchyard of St Thomas a Beckett in Heptonstall serving as the only memorial to a band of wicked men.

Clustered around the church of St John-in-the-Wilderness, the hamlet of Cragg has altered little since its days of infamy. Its people have changed, but its spectres linger on, tapping out their ethereal moidores as the light dims and as the scouring wind descends from Withens Moor. It may be only the knocking of a branch on a stone, or the plaintive trill of some distant curlew, but twilight in Cragg Vale can make you believe in ghosts.

Bibliography

The Strange Life of Charles Waterton Richard Aldington 1949

Fairs, Feasts and Frolics Julia Smith 1989

The Old Coaching Days in Yorkshire Tom Bradley 1889

Old Yorkshire edited by William Smith 1884

Annals of Yorkshire John Mayhall 1862

The History and Antiquities of Harewood John Jones 1859

Harry Ramsden (The Uncrowned King of Fish and Chips) Don Mosey and Harry Ramsden Junior 1989

Yorkshire Oddities (Incidents and Strange Events) S Baring Gould 1874

Portrait of West Yorkshire Margaret Slack 1984

Yorkshire's River Aire John Ogden 1976

Gleanings From Victorian Yorkshire Ian Dewhirst 1972

Legendary Yorkshire Frederick Ross 1872

Ackworth School Elfrida Vipont 1959

History of Spen Valley Douglas Hird 1985

Chronicles of Old Bingley Harry Speight 1898

Wakefield It's History and People J W Walker 1939

The Truth About Robin Hood P Valentine-Harris 1951

Bradford in History Horace Hird 1968

It's Odd — It's Yorkshire Arthur Gaunt 1971

Jowett 1921–1953 G I Garside 1985

Yorkshire Portraits Maria Hartley and Joan Ingilby 1961